CALL TO ORDER

CALL TO ORDER

A Miscellany of Useful Hierarchies, Systems, and Classifications

JACKIE STRACHAN & JANE MOSELEY

BLACK DOG
& LEVENTHAL
PUBLISHERS
NEW YORK

Black Dog & Leventhal Publishers
Hachette Book Group
1290 Avenue of the Americas
New York, NY 10104

www.hachettebookgroup.com

www.blackdogandleventhal.com

Originally published as *The Order of Things* in Great Britain by Robinson, an imprint of Little, Brown Book Group, a division of the Hachette UK Company in November 2017.

First American Edition: September 2018

Black Dog & Leventhal Publishers is an imprint of Running Press, a division of Hachette Book Group. The Black Dog & Leventhal Publishers name and logo are trademarks of Hachette Book Group, Inc.

The publisher is not responsible for websites (or their content) that are not owned by the publisher.

The Hachette Speakers Bureau provides a wide range of authors for speaking events. To find out more, go to www.HachetteSpeakersBureau.com or call (866) 376-6591.

Print book cover and interior design by Red Herring Design

Library of Congress Control Number: 2018902837

ISBNs: 978-0-316-48613-2 (Hardcover); 978-0-31648-612-5 (Ebook)

Printed in China

1010

10 9 8 7 6 5 4 3 2 1

CONTENTS

INTRODUCTION

When does the humble list become an established hierarchy? When it places things in order of importance, seniority, authority, value, priority, or status. Hierarchies create ranks and form boundaries, and thereby help us to impose order on our world. They can be relatively simple, top down or bottom up, or much more complex, with branches and subsections. They can apply to social, cultural, musical, religious, celestial, military, corporate, environmental, and biological contexts. The orders of things in this book range far and wide from the most obvious "I knew that," such as army and church ranks (in fact, the word *hierarchy* comes from the Greek word *hierarkhes*, meaning "sacred ruler"), to the "Who knew?" (such as typography and priority at sea, among many others). Many are man-made, the result of humans imposing structure—because that is what we like to do—and others help us make sense of the world; some are for fun (from the omega to the alpha male), while others still occur within the natural world (the food chains of different habitats).

The world in its infinite variety is hard enough to pin down in this manner as it is, and some of the pecking orders and hierarchies in this book also exist as variants according to the source, while some may be disputed by experts in the field. Hierarchies can be subjective, and that is their beauty.

SOCIETY IN THE EDO PERIOD

The social order in Japan during the Tokugawa or Edo period (1603–1867) under the shogunate founded by Tokugawa Ieyasu was structured around a rigid four-tier class system and was based on Confucian ideas. It was intended to create social harmony and stability, organizing society in part according to the contribution made by each level to the greater whole in a *"shi-no-ko-sho"* structure. Social mobility was extremely limited. The emperor and his family held the highest status, but the emperor wielded little actual power, relying heavily on the daimyos, the powerful nobles who were given land in return for their support. The most powerful daimyo became the shogun, governing the army and the country in general. During this period, the shoguns of the Tokugawa clan brought the daimyos under control.

The hierarchy was as follows, outside which were aristocrats, monastics, and outcasts.

WARRIOR CLASS OR SAMURAI (SHI)
Paid for by their daimyo to control the latter's domain, they were soldiers, government administrators, tax collectors, and generally wielders of great power, despite making up only a small percentage of the population.

TRAVEL BAN

During the Edo period the Japanese people were forbidden to travel abroad, and anyone who did so was not allowed to return. The result was a country that was virtually completely closed to the outside world until America made robust overtures in the 1850s.

At the bottom of the social order were the **BURAKUMIN**, which means "hamlet or village people." Their occupations were considered impure or associated with death or waste (butchers, tanners, undertakers, executioners). They were stigmatized as a result. Also known as *eta* (or "much filth"), they could be killed by members of the samurai if they had committed a crime. Other people lived outside this system entirely and were known as *hinin*. As "nonpersons," they survived by begging, and this section of society included beggars, prostitutes, and actors. The caste system was abolished in 1871 along with the feudal system.

FARMERS (NO)

The farmers fed and sustained the people and so were next in line of importance as vital members of society. This class embraced wealthy village heads, poorer tenant farmers, and those who owned no land at all.

ARTISANS (KO)

As manufacturers of useful products for society, using materials produced by others but for utilitarian purposes, the artisans were next in the order. Some artisans had rich patrons while others scraped out a living making simple baskets.

MERCHANTS (SHO)

Seen as the producers of nothing but instead as profiteers from the work of others, merchants had the lowest social status. Some members of this class would have their own stores while others sold goods on the streets.

EGYPTIAN SOCIETY

Egyptian society was structured rather like their famous pyramids. This "social pyramid" saw power held by a few at the apex, with the rest of the population descending in order of social status toward the slaves at the base. In the sky above was the pantheon of Egyptian gods led by Ra. The pharaohs were intermediaries between the gods and the people; they were the supreme leaders, exercising absolute power over their subjects. Class mobility was rare.

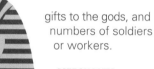

PHARAOH

Believed to be a god in human form, he/she made the laws and maintained order in the kingdom. Keeping the gods happy was a key part of the job.

GOVERNMENT OFFICIALS, NOBLES, AND PRIESTS

The vizier was the pharaoh's chief minister, second in command and sometimes serving as high priest. He was tasked with tax collection. Outside the royal family, only nobles could hold government posts, and they made local laws and generally kept order, profiting from tribute paid to the pharaoh by his subjects and donations made to the gods. Priests took on the day-to-day job of pleasing the gods.

SOLDIERS

Their role was to protect Egypt, control unrest, and supervise workers on the pyramids. Booty from battles was a perk of the job.

SCRIBES

Among the few literate people in Egypt, they were the record keepers, documenting events, gifts to the gods, and numbers of soldiers or workers.

MERCHANTS, ARTISANS, AND DOCTORS

The "middle class," including metalworkers, painters, potters, weavers, and stone carvers, who kept the country running.

FARMERS, SERVANTS, AND CONSTRUCTION WORKERS

The worker ants of Egyptian society, this group fed the kingdom, ensured their superiors' every whim was met, and built the pyramids and palaces. They included forced labor.

SLAVES

Chattel slaves were prisoners of war or those born of slave mothers. They included bonded laborers—those who sold themselves into slavery, for example, to clear a debt. The slaves worked in houses, quarries or mines, and temples, but in some respects they were on a par with servants, and life was often better for them than for their counterparts in other ancient civilizations.

THE ELIZABETHAN WORLD PICTURE

Elizabethan England was organized according to a hierarchical system known today as the Elizabethan World Picture. A "chain of being" linked the greatest to the least, with God at the very top of this chain, above the monarch, who ruled over all her subjects.

QUEEN ELIZABETH
Gloriana, God's representative on earth.

NOBILITY
The titles of peers were bestowed by the monarch or determined by birth, passed from father to oldest son. There were around fifty noble families, usually powerful landowners. In descending order of importance: duke and duchess, marquis and marchioness, earl and countess, viscount and viscountess, baron and baroness. (Archbishops held the same rank as dukes and bishops the same as earls.)

GENTRY
A class made up of, in descending order of importance, knights, squires, and gentlemen. Also landowners on a smaller scale; they were often very wealthy.

YEOMANRY
A kind of middle class that included farmers who owned or worked small parcels of land, merchants, tradesmen, and shopkeepers.

PEASANTS, LABORERS, AND SERVANTS
Non–land owning.

THE POOR, BEGGARS, AND PEOPLE UNABLE TO WORK
With the first rumblings of a rudimentary welfare system, the Poor Law made the parishes responsible for their poor, who were in turn classified as:

- Helpless poor, including the old, sick, and disabled.

- Able-bodied poor, who wanted to work but were unemployed.

- Rogues and vagabonds, able-bodied but more inclined to steal or beg than work.

THE ANT COLONY

Ants are eusocial creatures, meaning that they have a developed social structure and live in colonies with a strict caste system. Their life cycle involves four developmental stages: egg, larva, pupa, and adult, and it is during the larval stage that an ant's future is determined. Male ants have just one job to perform—to mate. The best-nourished female larvae will grow wings and become queens, whereas those who don't receive much TLC from the other ants become workers or soldiers. Additional worker castes (e.g., media or super soldiers) exist in some ant species, such as leaf cutters. Only the queen reproduces, and most of her offspring become workers and soldiers who collect food, protect the colony, and raise the young.

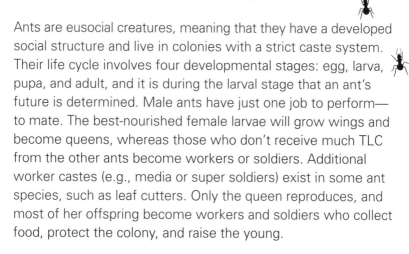

QUEEN
She may be top ant, but she doesn't order the other ants about; her sole role is to produce offspring. Depending on the species, a colony may have just one or multiple queens.

MALE
Born to mate with as many queens as possible and survive for the mating season only. A brief but very busy life.

NORMAL-SIZED WORKER
Worker ants are female and usually sterile; they forage, and build and defend the nest. A life of toil.

SOLDIER
Larger workers (may be equipped with swordlike jaws) that defend the colony. The fighting force of the ant world.

NURSE
Smaller workers who care for the larvae. Busy little bees, but not literally.

ROYAL LINES OF SUCCESSION

Historically, the question of who steps up when a monarch dies has often proved a bone of contention, leading to civil and even international wars. These days, however, it is far less chaotic. In the United Kingdom, home to what is generally acknowledged as the world's most famous monarchy, there are one hundred names on the royal line of succession list. But it is constantly evolving as new marriages are made and new babies (aka claimants) are born—and the rules changed radically when the Succession to the Crown Bill 2013 was introduced, putting an end to a centuries-old tradition of male primogeniture, whereby boys precede their elder sisters (if there are elder sisters) in the line.

The line directly descended from Queen Elizabeth II currently stands as follows:

1. **PRINCE CHARLES** (QUEEN'S ELDEST SON)

2. **PRINCE WILLIAM** (PRINCE CHARLES'S ELDER SON)

3. **PRINCE GEORGE** (PRINCE WILLIAM'S SON)

4. **PRINCESS CHARLOTTE** (PRINCE WILLIAM'S DAUGHTER)

5. **PRINCE HENRY, OR HARRY** (PRINCE CHARLES'S YOUNGER SON)

6. **PRINCE ANDREW** (QUEEN'S SECOND SON)

7. **PRINCESS BEATRICE** (PRINCE ANDREW'S ELDER DAUGHTER)

8. **PRINCESS EUGENIE** (PRINCE ANDREW'S YOUNGER DAUGHTER)

9. **PRINCE EDWARD** (QUEEN'S YOUNGEST SON)

10. **JAMES, VISCOUNT SEVERN** (PRINCE EDWARD'S SON)

11. **LADY LOUISE WINDSOR** (PRINCE EDWARD'S DAUGHTER)

12. **PRINCESS ANNE** (QUEEN'S DAUGHTER)

13. **PETER PHILLIPS** (PRINCESS ANNE'S SON)

14. **SAVANNAH PHILLIPS** (PETER PHILLIPS'S DAUGHTER)

15. **ISLA PHILLIPS** (PETER PHILLIPS'S DAUGHTER)

16. **ZARA TINDALL** (PRINCESS ANNE'S DAUGHTER)

17. **MIA GRACE TINDALL** (ZARA TINDALL'S DAUGHTER)

WE ARE NOT AMUSED

When English king Henry I's son and heir, William, died in a shipwreck in 1120, Henry made the unprecedented move of nominating his only other legitimate child—his daughter, Matilda—as his new heir. But despite Henry making his court swear an oath of loyalty to Matilda and her successors, it was Matilda's cousin, Stephen, who acceded, with the court's support, on Henry's death. Matilda was not amused, and the result was a civil war, known as the Anarchy, that lasted nearly twenty years.

PEERS OF THE REALM

There are five ranks in the English hereditary peerage, all conferred by the monarch. A peer of the realm may hold one or more titles from within these five ranks at the same time. The system evolved in feudal times, when men who swore an oath of loyalty to the monarch received protection or property in return. Modern peerages are created by letters patent under the Great Seal—the seal represents the sovereign's authority—rather than by the more dashing fastening of a ceremonial sword to the wearer's belt or girdle (cincture), as was the case for dukes and earls until 1615. Peerages in the top five ranks are hereditary. Most are passed on through the male line, but some pass on through heirs general, meaning they can pass down the female line.

Within each rank, precedent is established by the date the peerage was created: the earlier the date, the more senior the title bearer.

FIRST RANK
Duke

- Derives from the Latin *dux*, meaning "leader." Originally only kings were also dukes until kings began conferring dukedoms on their sons and favorites.

- The first English duke was created in 1337, when Edward III conferred the Dukedom of Cornwall on his son Edward of Woodstock, the Black Prince.

- Originally created by cincture, then by letters patent under the Great Seal.

- The first duke not a member of the royal family was Sir William de Pole, Marquess of Suffolk, who was made Duke of Suffolk in 1448.

- *Formal written address:* The Most Noble Duke of…

- *Spoken address:* Your Grace/His Grace.

- Any military, ecclesiastical, or ambassadorial rank is given first; for example, Major-General, the Duke of...

Royal Dukes

- A prince of royal blood is created duke either on his coming of age or marriage. Current royal dukes are Cambridge (Prince William), York (Prince Andrew), Gloucester (Prince Richard, grandson of George V), Edinburgh (Prince Philip) and Kent (Prince Edward, grandson of George V).

PUT UP YOUR DUKES

Some dukedoms can pass through the female line, in which case the title "duke" is retained. Queen Elizabeth II is also the Duke of Lancaster, as the title is always held by the reigning monarch.

Duchess

- The wife of a duke.

- *Formal written address:* The Most Noble Duchess of...

- *Spoken address:* Your Grace/ Her Grace.

SECOND RANK
Marquess/marquis

- A foreign import, introduced in 1385 by Richard II. It was never popular, especially among earls, whose status it usurped, and is little used now; the last new marquess to be conferred was in 1926.

- The first marquess was Robert de Vere, Earl of Oxford, who was made Marquess of Dublin in 1385.

- Conferred by letters patent under the Great Seal.

- *Formal written address:* The Marquess of...

- *Spoken address:* Your Lordship.

- Any military, ecclesiastical, or ambassadorial rank is given first; for example, Major-General, the Marquess of...

Marchioness

The wife of a marquess.

- *Formal written address:* The Marchioness of...

- *Spoken address:* Your Ladyship.

THIRD RANK
Earl

- Introduced to England by Danish king Canute (c. 994–1036); made hereditary under Norman rule.

- Originally created by cincture, then by letters patent under the Great Seal.

- *Formal written address:* The Right Honorable, the Earl of... (unless you are royal, in which case it is His Royal Highness, the Earl of...).

- *Spoken address:* Lord (name of earldom).

- Any military, ecclesiastical, or ambassadorial rank is given first; for example, Major-General, the Earl of...

Countess

- The wife of an earl.

- The female inheritor of an earldom.

- *Formal written address:* The Right Honorable, the Countess of…(unless you are royal, in which case it is Her Royal Highness, the Countess of…).

- *Spoken address:* Lady (name of earldom).

FOURTH RANK
Viscount

- The name derives from the Latin *vicecomes*, meaning "aide or lieutenant of a count."

- The first viscount was created in 1440 by Henry VI, king of both England and France, who elevated John, 6th Baron Beaumont, to the title of Viscount Beaumont of England and Viscount Beaumont of France.

- The title did not become popular until the seventeenth century.

- Conferred by letters patent under the Great Seal.

- *Formal written address:* The Right Honorable, the Viscount…

- *Spoken address:* Lord (name of viscountcy).

- Any military, ecclesiastical, or ambassadorial rank is given first: for example, Major-General, Viscount…

Viscountess

- The wife of a viscount.

- *Formal written address:* The Right Honorable, the Viscountess…

- *Spoken address:* Lady (name of viscountcy).

FIFTH RANK
Baron

- A baron was originally a land-owning tenant of the monarch. They were summoned by royal writ to attend Counsel or Parliament, like a kind of early House of Lords.

- In 1387, Richard II created the first baron by letters patent under the Great Seal. This was John Beauchamp de Holt, Baron Kidderminster.

- *Formal written address:* Lord (name of barony).

- *Spoken address:* Lord (name of barony).

- Any military, ecclesiastical, or ambassadorial rank is given first; for example, Major-General, Lord (name of barony)…

Baroness

- The wife of a baron.

- A baroness in her own right.

- *Formal written address:* Lady (name of barony).

- *Spoken address:* Lady (name of barony).

COURTESY TITLE
The son and heir apparent of a duke, marquess, or earl may use one of his father's titles as long as it is of a lesser grade. First sons of marquesses and earls take the courtesy title of viscount.

FREEMASONS

An international and historically secret society established to provide mutual help and fellowship among its members, who meet as equals, whatever their background. The first recorded initiation of a freemason is dated October 16, 1646, but the society's origins are thought to lie with a guild of stonemasons established in the late eleventh century in Europe. Skilled masons were highly sought after and, unlike serfs, were able to travel around practicing their art—hence, they were "free" masons. Fraternity "lodges" were formed, and in 1717 four London lodges met at an alehouse, the Goose and the Gridiron, united, and declared themselves a Grand Lodge—the world's first—with a Grand Master.

The Freemasons are famed for their elaborate ceremonies at which new members are admitted and for the annual installation of the Master and officers of the Lodge. Collar "jewels" are worn to denote the rank of the wearer, which is also indicated by where they sit in the Lodge. There are two levels of officer: progressive (who move up a rank each year) and nonprogressive.

PROGRESSIVE OFFICERS
Worshipful Master
The highest honor a Lodge can bestow. The Master sits in the east end of the Lodge and usually conducts the Lodge ceremonies.

Senior and Junior Warden
Both assist the Master in running the Lodge. The Senior Warden sits opposite the Master at the west end of the Lodge, and the Junior Warden at the south.

Senior and Junior Deacon
The deacons accompany the candidates during the ceremonies of the Three Degrees (Entered Apprentice, Fellow Craft, Master Mason). They each carry a wand as a badge of office.

Inner Guard
Sits just inside the door of the Lodge to check that only qualified persons enter.

Steward
Main function is to assist at the post-meeting dinner.

NONPROGRESSIVE OFFICERS
Immediate Past Master (IPM)
Sits on the left of the Worshipful Master and acts as his guide and support.

Chaplain
Leads the prayers at the beginning and end of each meeting.

Treasurer
Responsible for the Lodge finances and for recommending the amount of the annual subscription.

Secretary
Deals with the administration of the Lodge, including organizing meetings and distributing the agenda.

Director of Ceremonies (DC)
Oversees the ceremonies, including rehearsals, and ensures that the ceremonies are conducted with decorum.

Almoner
The Lodge welfare officer, with an in-depth knowledge of resources for those in need.

Charity Steward
Organizes charity collections and makes suggestions as to which charities to support.

Assistant Director of Ceremonies (ADC)
As the name suggests, the ADC assists the DC...

Assistant Secretary
...while the Assistant Secretary assists the Secretary.

Tyler
Usually stationed outside to guard the Lodge entrance and prevent any unwanted people from entering. Historically, handshakes or "tokens" and passwords were used to identify legitimate visitors.

Organist
Provides the music for meetings and ceremonies.

ROLLED-UP TROUSER LEG—FACT OR FICTION?
In some lodges one-act plays are staged during initiation and progression to a higher level, and postulant masons roll up a trouser leg to demonstrate they are free men, and not wearing a shackle.

WHO EATS WHOM?

Who preys on whom in the natural order of things? Few food chains are exclusive—although often specialized in their diets, most creatures consume more than one type of food, hence individual food chains interrelate to form a complex food web.

PRIMARY PRODUCERS—AUTOTROPHS
Self-sufficient organisms that make their own nutrients, such as plants through photosynthesis and bacteria through chemosynthesis.

PRIMARY CONSUMERS—HERBIVORES
Animals that eat primary producers.

SECONDARY CONSUMERS—PRIMARY CARNIVORES
Carnivores that eat herbivores.

TERTIARY CONSUMERS—SECONDARY CARNIVORES
Large carnivores that eat primary carnivores. They are usually larger and faster than primary carnivores.

QUATERNARY CONSUMERS—APEX PREDATORS
They have no natural predators other than man. Lions, sharks, polar bears…

In charge of waste disposal, **DECOMPOSERS AND DETRITIVORES** complete the cycle, feeding on and breaking down organic material, turning it into nutrients to return to the soil and nourish plants.

■ **Decomposers:** organisms such as fungi and bacteria.

■ **Detritivores:** animals such as worms and dung beetles.

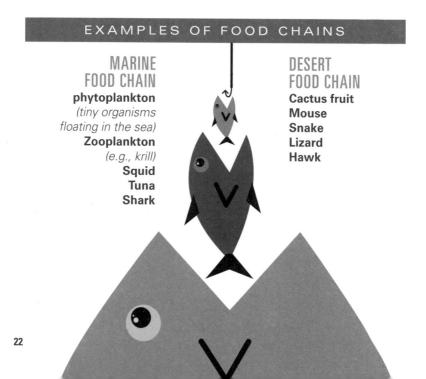

EXAMPLES OF FOOD CHAINS

MARINE FOOD CHAIN
phytoplankton
(tiny organisms floating in the sea)
Zooplankton
(e.g., krill)
Squid
Tuna
Shark

DESERT FOOD CHAIN
Cactus fruit
Mouse
Snake
Lizard
Hawk

FIVE STAGES OF GRIEF

Elisabeth Kübler-Ross, a Swiss psychiatrist, created a framework that describes the common stages a person goes through when grieving, such as when they are diagnosed with a terminal illness or when they lose a loved one. Since its publication in her book *On Death and Dying*, Kübler-Ross has clarified that not everyone goes through these stages, and some may experience two of phases at once, miss one altogether, or have two phases overlap.

DENIAL
During denial, the person often goes numb and, as a defense mechanism, refuses to believe the tragedy occurred or believes that the diagnosis is wrong, cling-ing to a delusional view of reality.

ANGER
When the reality of the situation sets in, a person reacts with anger to the unfairness of the situation, asking, "Why me?" and perhaps blaming others or questioning their religion.

BARGAINING
After anger, a person may try to negotiate their way out of the situation, saying, for example, "God, if you save my child, I will be a better person."

DEPRESSION
Finally, a person reaches the most recognizable form of grief: depression. In this stage, a per-son may cry, avoid others, and sink into despair.

ACCEPTANCE
The final stage is when a person comes to terms with the tragedy and emotions begin to stabilize.

THE MALE OF THE SPECIES

An unscientific look at the pecking order that operates loosely in the human male "pack."

ALPHA MALE
Mr. Big Guy, confident, charismatic, self-assured, dominant, driven, at ease socially, the life and soul of the party; natural leader, captain of industry, star of the soccer team, very successful with women.

BETA MALE
Mr. Nice Guy, Mr. Normal, less socially confident and more submissive than Alphas, with whom he tends to spend time, more reserved and moderate; good middle manager and good friend for women.

GAMMA MALE
Mr. My-Own-Guy, self-reliant, self-motivated, follows his own path, doesn't hang around Alpha or Beta males; thinkers, artists, and hipsters, successful with women.

DELTA MALE
Mr. Introvert, private, withdrawn, subordinate, crowd-pleasing; service provider, mostly unsuccessful with women.

SIGMA MALE
Mr. Lone Wolf, outrider and outsider in society, quiet but not shy, unconventionally clever, an introverted Alpha; surprisingly successful with women.

OMEGA MALE
Mr. Low Status, lacking in drive, socially awkward, shirks responsibility; often rejected by women. Omega is the twenty-fourth and final letter of the Greek alphabet.

TAXONOMY OF THE LIVING WORLD

Philosopher, scientist, and all-round intellectual Aristotle was the first to attempt to classify organisms in the fourth century BC. He classified plants and animals according to their similarities, grouping together those animals that lived on land, those in water, and those in the air. But it was eighteenth-century Swedish botanist Carl Linnaeus who really blazed a trail for taxonomy, and his system is still in use today, albeit with some changes. As methods for scientific investigation improve and new discoveries are made, it seems that nothing is set entirely in stone—some classifications are even now hotly disputed— and his system could be tweaked again or even reinvented further down the line.

Here are two basic examples from the Linnaean system.

	CAT	ROSE
Domain	Eukarya	Eukarya
Kingdom	Animalia	Plantae
Phylum	Chordata	Magnoliophyta
Class	Mammalia	Magnoliopsida
Order	Carnivora	Rosales
Family	Felidae	Rosaceae
Genus	*Felis*	*Rosoideae*
Species	*Felis catus*	*Rosa L.*

In *Rosa L.* above, "L" is for Linnaeus, who described it in his *Species Plantarum*, published in 1753. The binomial system gives species a two-part Latin name: genus (e.g., *Homo*) + species (e.g., *sapiens*). Some of the classifications can be divided further, into subphylum and infraphylum, and so on.

DOMAINS

American microbiologist Carl Woese proposed the three-domain system in 1977 to differentiate between cellular life forms: Archaea, Bacteria, and Eukarya. Both Archaea and Bacteria comprise simple single-celled microorganisms with no distinct nucleus, while Eukarya are advanced complex organisms, with cells that possess clearly defined nuclei, including plants and animals. Eukarya subdivides into kingdoms.

MOHS SCALE OF MINERAL HARDNESS

A ten-point scale of the hardness of minerals, based on one mineral's capacity to scratch a softer material so that the scratches can be seen by the naked eye. All minerals can be measured against the Mohs scale and assigned a hardness. For example, gold comes in on the scale at 2.5–3. Minerals can also measure below 1 or be off the scale beyond 10.

MOHS HARDNESS MINERAL CHEMICAL FORMULA

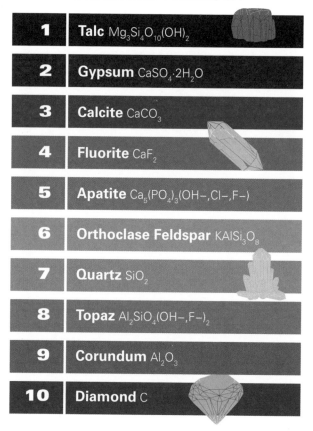

1	**Talc** $Mg_3Si_4O_{10}(OH)_2$	
2	**Gypsum** $CaSO_4 \cdot 2H_2O$	
3	**Calcite** $CaCO_3$	
4	**Fluorite** CaF_2	
5	**Apatite** $Ca_5(PO_4)_3(OH-,Cl-,F-)$	
6	**Orthoclase Feldspar** $KAlSi_3O_8$	
7	**Quartz** SiO_2	
8	**Topaz** $Al_2SiO_4(OH-,F-)_2$	
9	**Corundum** Al_2O_3	
10	**Diamond** C	

The scale was devised in 1812 by Friedrich Mohs, a German geologist and mineralogist, while he was working for Archduke Johann of Austria.

MERINO WOOL

Merino wool is graded according to the diameter of the fiber, crimp, yield, color, and staple strength, but the fineness is the most important factor in determining its quality and price. The wool is most prized as it is so fine, soft, and comfortable against the skin. Its microscopic diameter is about one-third to one-tenth the thickness of human hair. Fine yarns are used for fabrics and knitting yarns, whereas medium wool is used in woven cloths, knitting yarns, and furnishings. Broad wool is more durable and therefore used to make carpets and furnishings. The Micron system uses microns (equal to 1/1,000 of a millimeter, or 1/1,000,000 of a meter) to measure the diameter of a wool fiber.

MERINO WOOL GRADES

GRADE					
EXTRA FINE	ULTRA FINE	SUPER FINE	FINE	MEDIUM	BROAD
MICRON					
14.5 and finer	14.6–15.5	15.6–18.5	18.6–20.5	20.6–22.5	over 22.6

THE PH SCALE

The pH scale indicates how acidic or alkaline a substance is. It is a measure of the concentration of hydrogen (H) ions compared to that in distilled water. The scale ranges from 0 to 14. A pH of 7 is neutral. Pure water is neutral. A pH less than 7 is acidic. A pH greater than 7 is alkaline. The scale works logarithmically, so that each whole value below or above pH 7 is ten times more acidic or alkaline than the next one up (or down). So, a substance rated pH 3 is ten times more acidic than one rated pH 4, and 100 times more than pH 5. The scale was first devised in 1909 by Danish chemist Søren Sørensen (1868–1939)—while working for the Carlsberg Institute researching the chemistry of their beer—and revised in 1924. Examples are given below for each level.

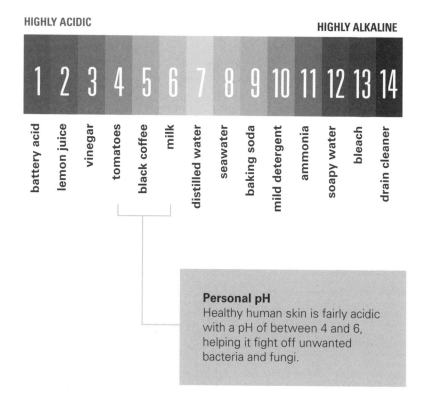

HIGHLY ACIDIC

HIGHLY ALKALINE

1 2 3 4 5 6 7 8 9 10 11 12 13 14

battery acid | lemon juice | vinegar | tomatoes | black coffee | milk | distilled water | seawater | baking soda | mild detergent | ammonia | soapy water | bleach | drain cleaner

Personal pH
Healthy human skin is fairly acidic with a pH of between 4 and 6, helping it fight off unwanted bacteria and fungi.

THE SCOVILLE SCALE

The heat of chiles is measured in SHUs (Scoville Heat Units)—the higher the number, the hotter the chile. The Scoville Unit is named for Wilbur Scoville, an American pharmacist who in 1912 devised a method of measuring the comparative heat of various chile peppers. Chiles, or the capsaicin they contained, were an important pharmaceutical ingredient.

The Scoville Method is based on dilution. One grain (65 milligrams) of ground chili is left overnight in 100cc of alcohol. The solution is then progressively diluted with sugar water. Trained tasters sample the solution at each dilution, until the heat of the chili can no longer be detected. Each dilution equals one SHU (Scoville Heat Unit); the stronger the chili, the more dilutions needed to reduce it to zero—the uber-eyewatering Carolina Reaper needs to be diluted as many as 2.2 million times to get to zero. Pure capsaicin measures 16,000,000 on the Scoville scale.

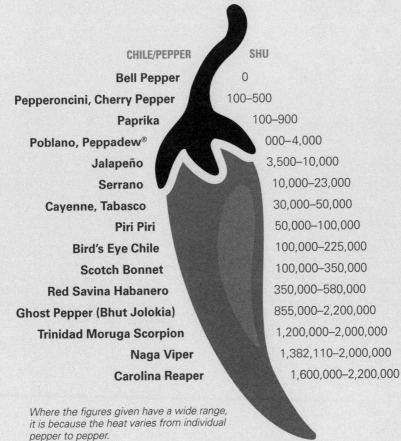

CHILE/PEPPER	SHU
Bell Pepper	0
Pepperoncini, Cherry Pepper	100–500
Paprika	100–900
Poblano, Peppadew®	000–4,000
Jalapeño	3,500–10,000
Serrano	10,000–23,000
Cayenne, Tabasco	30,000–50,000
Piri Piri	50,000–100,000
Bird's Eye Chile	100,000–225,000
Scotch Bonnet	100,000–350,000
Red Savina Habanero	350,000–580,000
Ghost Pepper (Bhut Jolokia)	855,000–2,200,000
Trinidad Moruga Scorpion	1,200,000–2,000,000
Naga Viper	1,382,110–2,000,000
Carolina Reaper	1,600,000–2,200,000

Where the figures given have a wide range, it is because the heat varies from individual pepper to pepper.

WEIGHT WATCHERS

Founded in the early 1960s by Jean Nidetch, the Weight Watchers diet doesn't require counting calories, but rather uses a SmartPoints® system that assigns a point level for every food based on its sugar, fat, and protein content. There is a limit to how many points a person can have per day based on their height, weight, and gender.

The Weight Watchers system allows a person to eat whatever they want—be it breads or pizza or even chocolate—but with the understanding that foods with higher points can only be consumed in smaller quantities to stay within the allotted daily points. A person can eat as many 0-point foods as they want, like fruits, veggies, and skinless chicken, as long as they aren't prepared with other ingredients like oil and sauces.

POINT VALUES FOR FOOD

25–10 Points sandwich, pizza, Caesar salad

8–7 Points hamburger, chocolate, whole milk, bagel with cream cheese

6 Points Coca-Cola, rice, orange juice

5 Points beer, potato, butter, veggie Subway sandwich

4 Points beef, ice cream sandwich, Starbucks cappuccino with nonfat milk

3–1 Points bread, apple and peanut butter, bean soup

0 Points apples, arugula, banana, beans, berries, broccoli, carrots, cauliflower, eggs, chicken breast, fish, grapes, corn

POINTS PER DAY BY WEIGHT

Weight	Points
<150 lbs.	**18 to 23 points**
150 to 174 lbs.	**20 to 25 points**
175 to 199 lbs.	**22 to 27 points**
200 to 224 lbs.	**24 to 29 points**
225 to 249 lbs.	**26 to 31 points**
250 to 274 lbs.	**28 to 33 points**
275 to 299 lbs.	**29 to 34 points**
300 to 324 lbs.	**30 to 35 points**
325 to 349 lbs.	**31 to 36 points**
> 350 lbs.	**32 to 37 points**

THE KITCHEN BRIGADE

A military unit in microcosm, it may come as no surprise to learn that the chain of command in a professional kitchen, as developed by Auguste Escoffier in the late nineteenth century, was based on his experience of the French army. Variations can be seen in the professional kitchens of large and small establishments across the world, with some roles being combined where a smaller team is employed. The hierarchy makes the role and authority of each member very clear. Kitchens have been compared to fields of battle…

CHEF DE CUISINE (KITCHEN CHIEF)
The "kitchen chief" is in overall charge of the kitchen, supervising staff, including apprentices, hygiene, menus, recipes, and the procurement of raw ingredients. Also known in some restaurants as the executive chef, and in larger establishments this is a separate role at the very top of the hierarchy.

SOUS-CHEF DE CUISINE (DEPUTY)
Reports to the chef de cuisine for the management of the kitchen.

CHEF DE PARTIE (SENIOR CHEF)
Manages a station in the kitchen where particular dishes are prepared.

CUISINIER/CUISINIER DE PARTIE (COOK)
Usually prepares specific dishes in a station in an independent role.

COMMIS (JUNIOR COOK)
Also works in a specific station and reports to the chef de partie.

APPRENTI(E) (APPRENTICE)
Helps with preparation and cleaning in all the various stations in order to gain practical experience while studying.

PLONGEUR (DISHWASHER)
Washes dishes and utensils but may also help with food preparation. In larger kitchens there is also a dedicated pot-and-pan washer (marmiton).

ABOYEUR (ANNOUNCER/EXPEDITER)
Charged with accepting orders from the restaurant and relaying them to the appropriate kitchen station.

TOURNANT (SPARE HAND)
Moves around helping at various stations.

COMMUNARD (STAFF COOK)
Prepares the meals served to the staff, also known as the family meal.

GARÇON DE CUISINE (KITCHEN BOY)
Supports the team in larger establishments, helping with preparation and other duties.

PÂTISSIER (PASTRY COOK):
Prepares baked items, desserts, and sweets (and sometimes breads). This role can also be broken down into other areas of specialization:

- **Boulanger** (baker): Prepares unsweetened dough.

- **Confiseur** (confectioner): Prepares candies and petit fours.

- **Glacier** (ice cream maker): Prepares cold and frozen desserts.

- **Décorateur:** Responsible for showpieces and special cakes.

BOUCHER (BUTCHER):
Butchers meat, poultry and sometimes fish.

SAUCIER (SAUCE MAKER / SAUTÉ COOK):
Prepares sauces and sautéed items. A key position.

RÔTISSEUR (ROAST COOK):
In charge of the team that cooks roasts and deep-fried dishes.

GRILLARDIN (GRILL COOK):
Prepares grilled foods.

FRITURIER (FRY COOK):
Prepares fried foods in place of the rôtisseur.

POISSONNIER (FISH COOK):
Prepares fish and seafood dishes.

ENTREMETIER (ENTRÉE PREPARER):
A combination of potager and legumier, prepares vegetable soups and stocks (and other vegetable dishes).

- **Potager** (soup cook): Prepares soups and reports to the entremetier.

- **Legumier** (vegetable cook): Prepares vegetable dishes and also reports to the entremetier.

GARDE MANGER (PANTRY OR COLD-FOODS CHEF):
In charge of cold foods, hors d'oeuvres, appetizers, buffets, and all kinds of charcuterie items.

WINE CLASSIFICATION

There have been many attempts at classifying wine over the ages—by country or region of origin, by grape variety, by vinification method, by vintage, even by sweetness, while most restaurant menus list bottles more prosaically by color and price. The European Union usually classifies wine made in its member countries by appellation, a French term that indicates the wine's region of origin and guarantees standards of grape variety used and winemaking techniques. The top four wine-producing countries in the EU are France, Italy, Spain, and Germany. From the humblest to the best, their individual classification systems are as follows:

FRANCE

VSIG (VIN SANS INDICATION GÉOGRAPHIQUE) / **VIN DE FRANCE**
Replaces the old *vin de table* (table wine) designation. The grape variety and even year may be specified, but the region is not given. Simple wines for everyday drinking.

IGP (INDICATION GÉOGRAPHIQUE PROTÉGÉE)
Wine with a stated geographical origin but made to less strict specifications than AOC/AOP. It is starting to replace the old *vin de pays* (country wine) designation, although this is still also used.

AOP (APPELLATION D'ORIGINE PROTÉGÉE) / **AOC** (APPELLATION D'ORIGINE CONTRÔLÉE)
AOP is a European designation for the top-quality wines. Wines made in specific regions, from particular grape varieties, and conforming to strict regulations. The French equivalent is AOC (*appellation d'origine contrôlée*), which is still also used, or AC (*appellation contrôlée*).

LETTERS OF THE LAW
Wines previously categorized as VDQS (*vin délimité de qualité supérieure*) must now either qualify as AOP/AOC or be downgraded to IGP.

DEUTSCHER TAFELWEIN
(GERMAN TABLE WINE)
A wine mostly for local consumption that must comply with only a few restrictions. A lesser-quality wine that may also be used for blending.

DEUTSCHER LANDWEIN
(GERMAN COUNTRY WINE)
A minimum of 0.5 percent more alcohol than Tafelwein; produced from one of a number of specified districts.

QUALITÄTSWEIN BESTIMMTER ANBAUGEBIETE (QBA)
A quality wine from a specific region or appellation that must comply with regulations (must be from a single wine-growing region, using approved grape varieties). May be chaptalized (sugar is added before fermentation to increase the alcohol).

PRÄDIKATSWEIN (PREVIOUSLY QUALITÄTSWEIN MIT PRÄDIKAT, QMP)
Wines of special distinction (not chaptalized) divided into several categories, with increasing levels of sugar as follows:

Kabinett
Usually a light wine. Dry, medium-dry, or sweet.

Spätlese (late harvest)
A superior-quality wine and more intense in flavor, made from grapes picked after the normal harvest. Dry, medium-dry, or sweeter.

Auslese (select harvest)
Often similar to a dessert wine, although it can be dry, medium-dry, or sweet.

Beerenauslese (berry selection)
Rich, sweet dessert wines.

Eiswein (ice wine)
Made from grapes that have frozen while still on the vine and affected by the *botrytis* fungus (noble rot). Very concentrated sweet wines with high acidity. Made in small amounts only, as Eiswein is reliant on the right weather conditions and the grapes being picked at the right moment. *Eiswein durch Technik!*

Trockenbeerenauslese
(dry berries selection)
From specially selected grapes picked when they have dried on the vine almost to raisins. Rich, sweet, and luscious.

VDT (VINO DA TAVOLA)
Table wine. Cheap, simple local wines for local consumption.

IGT (INDICAZIONE GEOGRAFICA TIPICA)
Wine that is typical of its geographical region (the focus is not on grape variety). Usually fairly basic but reasonable wines to be drunk young. Most of the

good-quality "Super Tuscans"—
red wines from Tuscany that do
not adhere to the strict DOC or
DOCG rules—are in this category.

DOC (DENOMINAZIONE DI ORIGINE
CONTROLLATA)
Made according to specific rules
(over three hundred appellations
all with their own rules). DOCs
of consistently high quality are
promoted to DOCG.

DOCG (DENOMINAZIONE DI ORIGINE
CONTROLLATA E GARANTITA)
Guaranteed to be made according
to strict rules to a very high
standard, from permitted grape
varieties. Sealed with a numbered
governmental stamp across the
cork as a guarantee of authenticity.

SPAIN

VDM (VINO DE MESA)
Table wine that does
not specify a region
or grape variety.

VDLT (VINO DE LA TIERRA)
"Wine of the land."
Regional wines that are
not produced in DO-
designated areas and
do not follow strict
regulations. They can
offer good quality
and value for money.

VCIG (VINOS DE CALIDAD CON
INDICACIÓN GEOGRÁFICA)
Quality wines with geographical
indication. After five years at this
level, a VCIG wine may apply for
DO status.

DO (DENOMINATION DE ORIGEN)
Designation of origin. Good-
quality wines from over sixty
different designated regions
that must comply with strict
standards. Over half the total
wine-growing area of Spain
produces DO wines.

DO PAGO (VINO DE PAGO)
Single-estate wines with an
excellent reputation but unable
to claim DO status, for example,

due to being outside the catch-
ment area. Allowed to set their
own regulations for production.

DOC/DOCA (DENOMINACIÓN
DE ORIGEN CALIFICADA)
Appellation of origin. The most
strict classification producing the
highest-quality Spanish wines. To
date only the Rioja and Priorat (in
Catalonia, where the designation
is DOQ) regions have this classification.

WINE AGING CLASSIFICATION

JOVEN
Wines under fifteen
months old.

CRIANZA
Aged for at least two
years.

RESERVA
Aged for at least three
years.

GRAN RESERVA
Aged for at least five
years.

CHAMPAGNE BOTTLES

A standard champagne bottle contains 75 cl of champagne, or approximately six to eight glasses of champagne, depending on the size of your glass or flute. Other sizes are available with increasingly exotic names, but anything above a Nebuchadnezzar is usually made to order for special occasions.

SIZE MATTERS

The smaller the bottle, the quicker the champagne inside it will age. This is because the neck size for a quart, demie, standard, or magnum of champagne is the same, so the air-to-wine ratio is smaller in a magnum than in, say, a demie, so champagne ages more slowly in a bigger bottle.

BIBLICAL BUBBLES

Most bottles larger than a magnum are named for Old Testament kings of Israel—Balthazar, for example, was one of the three Magi. No one really knows why the bottles are so named, although there is much speculation. They were all men of worth, standing, and importance; perhaps the champagne makers wanted to confer some gravitas on their product.

Quart 20 cl
quarter standard bottle

Demie 37.5 cl
half standard bottle

Standard 75 cl

Magnum 150 cl
2 standard bottles

Jeroboam 300 cl
4 standard bottles

Rehoboam 450 cl
6 standard bottles

Methuselah 600 cl
8 standard bottles

Salmanazar 900 cl
12 standard bottles

Balthazar 1,200 cl
16 standard bottles

Nebuchadnezzar 1,500 cl
20 standard bottles

SPECIAL-OCCASION BOTTLES

Solomon 1,800 cl
24 standard bottles

Sovereign 2,625 cl
35 standard bottles*

Primat or Goliath 2,700 cl
36 standard bottles

Melchizedek 3,000 cl
40 standard bottles

Made just once by Taittinger in 1988 for the launch of the world's then biggest cruise ship, The Sovereign of the Seas.

MICHELIN STARS

In 1900 the Michelin tire company published its first guidebook, a book with a blue cover given free to motorists with information on garages, accommodation, and meals to encourage people to travel around France. In 1926 the company sent anonymous reviewers to try out the country's various restaurants and submit their feedback, and in that year the first star was awarded. The three-star system was inaugurated five years later. The anonymity and meticulous documentation continue today, and after detailed reports are carefully reviewed and discussed in lengthy meetings between inspectors and the guide's editors, stars are awarded, retained, or lost.

Bib Gourmand restaurants were introduced in 1997—and are also listed in the Michelin guidebooks. "Bib" comes from the "Michelin Man" logo, known as "Bibendum." The restaurants are listed in the standard Michelin Guides (the famous *Guides Rouges* / Red Guides) and in their own dedicated guide, *Les Bonnes Petites Tables du Guide Michelin.*

THREE STARS
Exceptional cuisine, worth a special journey.

TWO STARS
Excellent cooking, worth a detour.

ONE STAR
High-quality cooking, worth a stop.

BIB GOURMAND
Good-quality, good-value cooking.

The focus is on the quality of the ingredients, on skill in preparation, and in combining flavors, with the personality of the chef conveyed through their cuisine, consistency of standards, and value for money. Less emphasis is placed on décor and quality of service. Restaurants under consideration for stars are visited several times a year. France tops the charts as the country with the most stars, but Tokyo leads the way as the city with the most three-starred restaurants.

ZAGAT

The New York–based dining guide *Zagat*, established in 1979, used to operate a thirty-point system for reviews based on food, décor, and service and using ratings from restaurant goers. It now scores restaurants on a sliding scale from one to five stars, taking into account online ratings and reviews, feedback from the public, and diners on the ground to award points. The guide covers the USA, London, Toronto, and Vancouver.

4.6–5.0 stars Extraordinary to perfection
4.1–4.5 stars Very good to excellent
3.1–4.0 stars Good to very good
2.1–3.0 stars Fair to good
1.0–2.0 stars Poor to fair

THE DANISH SMILEY SYSTEM

Retail food enterprises in Denmark must comply with food regulations and are inspected, unannounced, between one and three times a year. In 2001 Smiley reports were introduced, with smiley symbols awarded according to findings. In 2008 the "Elite Smiley" came into being, awarded to those enterprises with four consecutive happy smiles in their inspection reports and no adverse comments in the previous twelve months. Customers can view the pictorial ratings in supermarkets, restaurants, bakeries, butchers, grocery stores, hot dog stands, school cafeterias, nursing homes, and hospital kitchens, and make informed choices about where to shop and eat. The smiles range from a very happy to a sour face, and inspection reports are published on *findsmiley.dk*.

 The Elite Smiley is awarded to those with the best inspection history.

 No remarks.

 Issued with an enjoining order or warning.

 Issued with an injunction order or prohibition.

 Administrative penalties, reported to the police, or approval withdrawn.

TABLE ETIQUETTE

Modern formal dining in Western society is served *à la russe*. Courses are served in a fixed order from soup to dessert and coffee. This system is believed to have been introduced to France in the early nineteenth century by the Russian ambassador Prince Alexander Kurakin. It rapidly replaced the older system, service *à la française*, where all the dishes are put on the table at once. The new method imposed a hierarchy on the arrangement of cutlery/flatware, to help diners know in which order to use it. The general rule is to work from the outside in.

SETTING FOR A FOUR-COURSE MEAL

FROM LEFT TO RIGHT
fish fork, dinner fork, salad fork, charger plate, dinner/steak knife, fish knife, soup spoon

The oyster fork, if used, is placed to the right of the soup spoon, angled so that the tines rest in the spoon bowl.

Service *à la russe* saw the introduction of the menu, so that diners would know what they would be served as they could no longer see it spread out on the table.

GENERAL RULES

- Forks to the left, knives and spoons to the right.

- Knife blades face toward the plate.

- 15 inches / 38 centimeters elbow room between each place setting.

- Cutlery/flatware aligns with the bottom of the plate, 1 inch / 2.5 centimeters from the table edge.

- First item is 1 inch / 2.5 centimeters from the plate.

- No more than three utensils of the same type at any one time, with the exception of the oyster fork.

- Napkins are placed on the charger plate or to the left of the forks.

ABOVE AND SLIGHTLY TO LEFT OF FORKS
butter plate, butter knife placed diagonally, handle facing guest

ABOVE AND SLIGHTLY RIGHT OF KNIVES
water glass, white wine glass, red wine glass, champagne glass

ABOVE PLATE
dessert spoon (top), bowl facing left, dessert fork (below spoon), tines facing right (placed just before dessert is served, unless the main meal is only two courses)

CHARGER PLATE
This is a large plate that forms the base for the plates containing the first and fish courses; it is removed when the main course is served.

THE U.S. GOVERNMENT

THE CONSTITUTION
The oldest written national constitution (1787) still in use, it defines the framework of the U.S. federal government. The government is divided into three branches that are separate but equal to ensure no group or individual can gain too much control. Each branch can change/ overturn acts and laws issued by the other branches in a system of checks and balances.

LEGISLATIVE BRANCH
Makes laws, confirms/rejects presidential appointments, and has the authority to declare war.

Congress (and agencies that provide help to Congress)
Confirms/rejects the president's appointments; it can remove the president from office in exceptional circumstances.

Senate
American citizens vote for two senators per state (one hundred in total); they serve for a term of six years, but there is no limit to the number of terms a senator can serve.

House of Representatives
American citizens vote for 435 representatives, divided among

the fifty states proportionate to the state's population size. Representatives serve two-year terms with no limit to the number of terms.

EXECUTIVE BRANCH
Carries out and enforces laws.

President
The head of state, leader of the federal government, and commander in chief of the U.S. Armed Forces. The president serves a four-year term, for no more than two terms. The president can veto laws passed by Congress.

Vice President
Supports the president and assumes the presidency if the former is no longer able to serve. Can serve an unlimited number of four-year terms, although in practice no one has served more than two.

Cabinet
Cabinet members are nominated by the president (whom they advise) and are approved by the Senate. They include the vice president and the heads of fifteen executive departments. They are nominated by the president and must be approved by the Senate.

Other
Executive departments, independent agencies, boards, and committees that help carry out the decisions made by government.

JUDICIAL BRANCH
Interprets the meaning of laws, applies them to individual cases, decides if they violate the Constitution.

Supreme Court
Justices are appointed by the president and the Senate, and can overturn unconstitutional laws. The Supreme Court comprises the chief justice and eight associate justices. Justices are appointed for life, but may retire or be removed in exceptional circumstances.

Other federal courts
Congress has the authority to create other federal courts. They try cases such as the constitutionality of a law involving public ministers, disputes between states, and bankruptcy.

State courts
They try most criminal cases, probate, family law, tort, etc.

ALL THE PRESIDENT'S MEN

Should a president die, resign from, fail to qualify, be removed from, or become unable to discharge the powers and duties of office, the Constitution of the United States and Presidential Succession Act of 1947 have got it covered. Next in line is the vice president, and should something befall him or her, the baton passes to the Speaker of the House of Representatives. Stepping into the breach next is the president pro tempore of the Senate (the most senior member of the majority party), in whose potentially vacant footsteps would come the Cabinet members, with their eligibility based on the date their offices were established.

The Twenty-Fifth Amendment of the Constitution, ratified in 1967, allows the vice president to step into the presidential chair during illness or a temporary inability to fulfill duties. In 1985 Ronald Reagan put George H. W. Bush in charge when he underwent surgery.

POTENTIAL LINE OF SUCCESSION
vice president
Speaker of the House of Representatives
president pro tempore of the Senate
secretary of state
secretary of the treasury
secretary of defense
attorney general
secretary of the interior
secretary of agriculture
secretary of commerce
secretary of labor
secretary of health and human services
secretary of housing and urban development
secretary of transportation
secretary of energy
secretary of education
secretary of veterans affairs
secretary of homeland security

DESIGNATED SURVIVOR

In the event of a State of the Union address or a presidential inauguration, at which the president and all successors are due to be present, a "designated survivor" stays behind in a secure location.

GLADIATORIAL COMBAT

In the early days of the Roman Empire, slaves, prisoners of war, and criminals were forced to train in the gladiator schools to fight in the arena in front of the bloodthirsty crowds. Later in the empire's history, free men sometimes also enrolled, attracted by the prospect of glory and money if successful—gladiators ("swordsman," from *gladius*, "sword") could keep any prizes or gifts received during the games. A loose hierarchy evolved among them, based on experience and the sheer ability to stay alive, and to an extent upon the type of fighting in which they specialized.

RUDIARIUS

Elite gladiators who had fought so bravely and well that they had obtained their freedom. They could retire completely or work in some capacity, often as a bodyguard or training other gladiators, or they could choose to carry on in the arena, soaking up the adulation of the mob. A *rudiarius* could never become a Roman citizen, although his children could.

PRIMUS PALUS

A top-ranking gladiator. *Primus palus* translates as "first pole." The gladiators trained by slashing at poles (*pali*) fixed in the ground.

SECUNDUS PALUS

A second-ranking gladiator, or "second pole"; followed by "third pole," "fourth pole," and so on.

VETERANUS

A gladiator who had survived his first fight.

TIRO

A trained novice gladiator deemed ready for his first fight.

NOVICIUS

A trainee gladiator.

GLADIATORS GOT TALENT

Gladiators were trained to fight in one of numerous different ways. Some combat specialists were regarded as more elite than others; for example, the *sagittarius*, a skilled bowman on horseback, who was popular with the crowd, unlike the hapless *retiarius*, who fought with a net, requiring evasive tactics that the crowd deemed unmanly. And some were more heavily armed (e.g., *hoplomachus*, with sword, dagger, and lance) than others (e.g., *lacquerarius*, with one weapon and a lasso). Differing specialists were paired specifically to produce an entertaining combat.

THE ROMAN SENATE

The Roman Republic was an ancient state that existed for nearly five hundred years, from 509 BC until the establishment of the Roman Empire in 27 BC. Its complex form of government, with a constitution of sorts, laws, and elected officials, bore a marked resemblance to modern democracies, although there were disparities based on social class, wealth, and gender (women could neither vote nor hold office). The Republic was run by a Senate headed by two consuls, all of whom were patricians—members of a noble family or class. However, there was considerable input from the Assembly, which comprised the plebeians, or commoners—the (male) citizens of Rome.

CONSULS

The Assembly elected the two consuls from the Senate by majority vote. Consuls served a one-year term; their duties were to oversee the work of other government officials, command the army, act as judges, and select a new Senate member in the event of a senator's death. In times of crisis requiring prompt action, the consuls could appoint a "dictator," who was in command until the crisis was resolved. Importantly, the consuls had to agree on decisions, and each had the power to veto the other—this overcame the risk of one consul taking total control.

PROCONSULS

A proconsul was a governor appointed by the Senate to rule provinces conquered by Rome, many of which were relatively far-flung. The proconsuls had much the same authority as the consuls.

THE SENATE

The three hundred members of the Senate (derived from the Latin *senex*, meaning "old man") were sandwiched between the consuls above them and the Assembly below, and advised both. They had the power to approve or disapprove laws proposed by the Assembly and make decisions on finance and foreign policy. Once elected, a senator was in post for life.

Specialist Senate posts included:

Praetors

Magistrates ranked immediately below the consuls, to whom they acted as deputy when necessary. They were also in charge of the judiciary and were responsible for staging the public games that were a feature of life in ancient Rome.

Censor

Official responsible for overseeing the census. He also had the power to promote or demote individuals with regard to social class.

Aediles

Officials responsible for the maintenance of public buildings and roads and the regulation of festivals.

Quaestors

Officials in charge of public revenue and expenditure.

THE ASSEMBLY

In addition to electing the two consuls, the Assembly—or Plebeian Council—elected government officials (including judges), voted on laws proposed by government officials (and vetoed them, if required, through representatives known as tribunes), and declared war or peace, as appropriate.

Ps & Qs

As the Roman Republic became established, plebeians were able to rise to higher ranks of office. For example, in 409 BC the first plebeian quaestor—the lowest-ranking magistrate—was appointed; in 356 BC the first plebeian dictator was appointed, later taking the position of censor; while 337 BC saw the elevation of a plebeian to the post of praetor.

LA COSA NOSTRA

With its origins in medieval Sicily, the organized crime of the Mafia began to take a foothold in the United States in the late nineteenth century. By the early 1930s, bolstered by the large number of Italian immigrants, the American Mafia had become tremendously powerful, ousting rival gangs and seizing control of their illegal activities. They adopted the name that would come to strike a chill in the heart of anyone not connected with "the family"—La Cosa Nostra, "Our Affair" or "Our Thing."

COMMISSION

Made up of the heads of the most powerful Mafia "families" or factions. Only the Commission can challenge the authority of a boss.

BOSS/DON

Head of the family, feared and very wealthy thanks to the "tribute," or cut, he receives from the entire family's earnings. He makes all the important decisions.

CONSIGLIERE

A trusted friend and confidant who acts as a counselor to the boss and a mediator in disputes.

UNDERBOSS

The powerful number two—often a direct blood family member— he is groomed to take over from the boss. He runs the family's day-to-day operations and receives a percentage earnings cut from the boss.

CAPOREGIME/CAPO

He carries out the orders of the boss and underboss, and is in charge of a crew of ten to twenty soldiers. He also acts as a buffer, distancing the boss from what otherwise may be a too-direct association with the family's activities.

SOLDATO/SOLDIER

One of the "boots on the ground" who carries out the family's dirty work—intimidation, extortion, murder...A "made man" who must be of Italian descent and take an oath of *omertà*—silence and noncooperation with the authorities.

ASSOCIATE

Not yet an official member of the Mafia, he runs errands and carries out small jobs for those above. An associate aspires to prove his worth and become a "made man."

THE TRIADS

A secret society that originated in China, today the triads are crime gangs that still work to strict rules with the swearing of an oath and a Mafia-like tradition of mutual assistance. They are active on an international scale, including in major cities in the UK, North America, Australia, and New Zealand. The triads use numeric codes based on Chinese numerology to differentiate between the ranks of their members and have a system of secret signs and tattoos through which they can communicate clandestinely.

SHAN CHU (489)
Mountain/Dragon Master
Group leader

FU SHAN CHU (438)
Deputy Mountain Master
Deputy leader

HEUNG CHU (438)
Incense Master
Performs initiation and promotion ceremonies and rituals.

SIN FUNG (438)
Vanguard
Recruits members, organizes and assists at ceremonies.

PAK TSZ SIN (415)
White Paper Fan
Administrative officer. Advises on business and finance.

HUNG KWAN (426)
Red Pole
Commands units of fifty men. Oversees offensive and defensive operations. Red Poles have a background in the military.

CHO HAI (432)
Straw Sandal or Glass Slipper
Organizes meetings and gang fights. Liaises between units.

49 CHAI
Ordinary gang member
New recruits and triad foot soldiers.

BLUE LANTERNS
Uninitiated members

THE KNIGHTS TEMPLAR

Members of a religious military order established to protect Christian Crusaders, the Knights Templar in their distinctive white surcoat with a red cross have become associated with legend and mystery. The Crusades, mounted to halt Muslim expansion into the Holy Land, began in 1095 and continued until the fall of the last Crusader stronghold in 1291, and thereafter, with rather less zeal, until the sixteenth-century Protestant Reformation heralded the decline of papal authority. However, the Order itself was annihilated in 1307, falsely accused of blasphemy by King Philip IV of France, who was in need of the Order's vast wealth. Many of its members were put through seven years of inquisition, followed by public execution.

GRAND MASTER
In overall charge of the Order worldwide. It was an elected office, held for life—that of the last Master, Jacques de Molay, came to a gruesome end when he was burned at the stake, declaring: "God will avenge our deaths."

MASTER AND COMMANDER
A local commander, in control of a small Templar stronghold known as a commandery.

SENESCHAL
The Master's right-hand man, who in peacetime administered the Order's lands and in wartime masterminded the practical stuff—moving men and their pack trains, and procuring food.

TURCOPOLIER
In command of the light cavalry and the sergeant brothers.

MARSHAL
In charge of arms and horses.

UNDERMARSHAL
In charge of the horses' tack.

STANDARD BEARER
In charge of the squires. Despite his name, he marched in front of the banner, rather than "bearing" it himself.

KNIGHT
Armor-clad and skilled in warfare, the knights were the backbone of the battlefield.

SERGEANT
A light cavalry officer, and support for the noble knights, usually of a lower social class. Sergeants wore a black or brown mantle over their black tunic, often with a red cross like the knights.

TREASURER
In charge of the books—a responsible position, as the Knights Templar were a very wealthy order.

DRAPER
In charge of clothing and bed linen.

SQUIRES
Assistants to the knights.

LAY SERVANTS
Their duties varied widely, depending on whose servant they were.

CHAPLAINS
A separate class from the knights, they were responsible for conducting religious services, administering the sacraments, and addressing the spiritual needs of the Templars.

UNLUCKY FOR SOME
Among the legends that have grown up around the Templars over the centuries are their associations with freemasonry, with the Holy Grail, and with Scotland—in particular with Rosslyn Chapel near Edinburgh. They have also been credited as the source of the unlucky day Friday the thirteenth—many were arrested in the Templar purge on Friday, October 13, 1307. And don't forget the legend of the lost Templar treasure that is still waiting to be found... somewhere.

ARMY	MARINES
Private (PV1)	Private (PvT)
Private (PV2)	Private First Class (PFC)
Private First Class (PFC)	Lance Corporal (LCpl)
Corporal (CPL), Specialist (SPC)	Corporal (Cpl)
Sergeant (SGT)	Sergeant (Sgt)
Staff Sergeant (SSG)	Staff Sergeant (SSgt)
Sergeant First Class (SFC)	Gunnery Sergeant (GySgt)
Master Sergeant (MSG), First Sergeant (1SG)	Master Sergeant (MSgt), First Sergeant (1st Sgt)
Sergeant Major (SGM), Command Sergeant Major (CSM), Sergeant Major of the Army (SMA)	Master Gunnery Sergeant (MGySgt), Sergeant Major (SgtMaj)
	Sergeant Major of the Marine Corps (SMMC)

U.S. MILITARY RANKS

The system of officer ranks is the backbone of an army's hierarchy. It makes clear the roles and responsibilities of each member. The three graphs that follow range from enlisted members (the lowest), to warrant officers, to commissioned officers.

NAVY	AIR FORCE
Seaman Recruit (SR)	Airman Basic (AB)
Seaman Apprentice (SA)	Airman (Amn)
Seaman (SN)	Airman First Class (A1C)
Petty Officer Third Class (PO3)	Senior Airman (SrA)
Petty Officer Second Class (PO2)	Staff Sergeant (SSgt)
Petty Officer First Class (PO1)	Technical Sergeant (TSgt)
Chief Petty Officer (CPO)	Master Sergeant (MSgt), First Sergeant (E-7)
Senior Chief Petty Officer (SCPO)	Senior Master Sergeant (SMSgt), First Sergeant (E-8)
Master Chief Petty Officer (MCPO), Force Command Master Chief Petty Officer (FORMC), Fleet Command Master Chief Petty Officer (FLTMC)	Chief Master Sergeant (CMSgt), First Sergeant (E-9), Command Chief Master Sergeant (CCM)
	Chief Master Sergeant of the Air Force (CMSAF)

OFFICER RANKING

Army, Air Force, Marines	Navy, Coast Guard
Second Lieutenant	Ensign
First Lieutenant	Lieutenant (Junior Grade)
Captain	Lieutenant
Major	Lieutenant Commander
Lieutenant Colonel	Commander
Colonel	Captain
Brigadier General	Rear Admiral (lower half)
Major General	Rear Admiral (upper half)
Lieutenant General	Vice Admiral
General	Admiral
General of the Army / Air Force *Marines do not have a corresponding rank.*	Fleet Admiral

WARRANT OFFICER*

Navy	Coast Guard	Army, Marines
Warrant Officer 1 (WO1) (discontinued)	Warrant Officer 1 (WO1)	Warrant Officer 1 (WO)
Chief Warrant Officer 2 (CWO2)	Chief Warrant Officer (CW2)	Chief Warrant Officer 2 (CWO2)
Chief Warrant Officer 3 (CWO3)	Chief Warrant Officer 3 (CW3)	Chief Warrant Officer 3 (CWO3)
Chief Warrant Officer 4 (CWO4)	Chief Warrant Officer 4 (CW4)	Chief Warrant Officer 4 (CWO4)
Chief Warrant Officer 5 (CWO5) *Navy only*	Chief Warrant Officer 5 (CW5)	Chief Warrant Officer 5 (CWO5)

*There are no warrant officers in the Air Force.

THE ROMAN ARMY

Although it changed over the centuries, for many people the archetypal Roman army of popular imagination is that of the post–Marian Reforms of 107 BC (military reforms initiated by general and statesman Gaius Marius), structured largely as follows (the exact numbers of troops per unit varies slightly according to source). It was a professional standing army of volunteers comprising around thirty legions.

Each legion had auxiliary units such as archers or cavalry attached to it. Soldiers performing special duties included a cornicen, who would sound a large circular trumpet to signal orders, and an aquilifer, who carried the legion's standard, representing its honor.

LEGIO (LEGION)
Comprised ten cohorts (nine + the double-strength First Cohort), totaling around 5,500 men. Commanded by a *legatus legionis*, assisted by various officers including several tribunes and a *praefectus castrorum* (camp prefect), a veteran soldier who was third in command of the legion (after the *legatus* and tribunus).

COHORS PRIMA (FIRST COHORT)
Comprised five double-size *centuriae*, therefore totaling eight hundred men, excluding officers. They included elite troops and specialists in some form of trade (blacksmiths, construction, etc.).

COHORTES I–IX (COHORTS 1–9)
Each comprised six *centuriae*, therefore totaling 480 men, excluding officers.

CENTURIA (CENTURY)
Comprised of ten *conturbenia*, therefore totaling eighty men, excluding officers. Commanded by a centurion, assisted by several officers, including the *optio*, second in command. The First Cohort's centurion was the *primus pilus* (first spear), the highest-ranking centurion in the legion.

CONTURBENIUM
The smallest unit, a group of eight soldiers who shared a tent. Commanded by a *decanus*.

THE ROMAN CATHOLIC CHURCH

Its name derived from the Greek word *katholikos*, meaning "universal," the Catholic Church dates its foundation to the Christian community established by Jesus. The Church was established in Rome by the apostle Peter, named "the Rock," as he would be the foundation upon which the Church was built. Jesus nominated Peter as the first pope, and all subsequent popes—265 to date—are considered Peter's successors. As the Church grew, it became necessary to appoint a clergy to act in persona Christi Capitis ("in the person of Christ, the Head [of the Church]"). The clergy—currently all male—is ordained through the Sacrament of Holy Orders and divided into the episcopate, the priesthood, and the deaconate.

THE EPISCOPATE

Pope

The Bishop of Rome, head of the Roman Catholic Church, and the only bishop who can speak on behalf of the entire Church. The pope's cathedral church is St. Peter's Basilica in the heart of Vatican City, the 44-hectare (109-acre) independent papal state in Rome.

Cardinal

Cardinals are nominated by the pope and form the Sacred College, responsible since 1059 for electing succeeding popes— prior to that, popes were elected by the clergy and laity of Rome. Since 1378, when Urban VI, a noncardinal, was elected, all popes have been elected from

THE DIACONATE
DEACON

The lowest rank of ordained minister who assists in preaching the Gospel, but, unlike those in the episcopate and priesthood, has no special charisma (divinely conferred power). A "transitional" deacon is one who intends to become a priest, while a "permanent" deacon will remain a deacon.

within the Sacred College. There are currently 223 cardinals worldwide, of which only 117 are electors, the remainder being over the age of eighty and therefore no longer eligible to vote.

Archbishop

The chief bishop (see below) of a diocese considered important because of its size and/or historical significance. In the Church of England, established in 1534, the archbishop of Canterbury is the equivalent of the pope in his role as senior bishop and principal leader of the Anglican Church (Canterbury has been the seat of Christianity in Britain since AD 597).

Bishop

A successor of the apostles and responsible for a diocese, made up of local parishes. Only bishops may confer the Sacrament of Holy Orders and consecrate chrism (sacramental oil).

THE PRIESTHOOD
Diocesan Priest

A coworker of a bishop and usually ordained by the bishop in whose diocese he will serve. A diocesan priest may be conferred with the title Monsignor, establishing the priest as a member of the papal household.

Vicar General

An assistant to the bishop, assisting in the governance of a diocese.

Archpriest or Vicar Forane

A priest in charge of a *vicariate forane* (a group of parishes within a diocese), who assists the priests of those parishes.

Parish Priest or Pastor

Responsible for the pastoral care of the laity in a parish within the diocese.

Parochial Vicar

An assistant to a parish priest.

PAPAL CONCLAVE

Cardinals electing a new pope gather in the Sistine Chapel in the Apostolic Palace, the pope's official residence, where they vote for their favored candidate. A candidate requires two-thirds of the vote to ascend, and the process doesn't always go smoothly—in 1378, for example, failure to agree led to the Western Schism, a split within the Catholic Church that lasted until 1417.

THE CHURCH OF ENGLAND

The Protestant Church of England was established when King Henry VIII broke with the Roman Catholic Church in order to divorce his wife, Catherine of Aragon (who had failed to produce a male heir to the throne), and marry Anne Boleyn (who also failed to produce a male heir, but that's another story...). In 1534 Henry passed the Act of Supremacy, which recognized him as the "only supreme head of the Church of England called *Anglicana Ecclesia.*" His daughter Queen Elizabeth I declared herself Supreme Governor of the Church of England, a title passed down through the royal line of succession and today held by Queen Elizabeth II. The Church is divided into areas of ever-decreasing size, as follows:

PROVINCE
There are two provinces, south and north. The south is led by the Archbishop of Canterbury and the north by the Archbishop of York.

DIOCESE OR SEE
A large area under the authority of a bishop. The word *see* is derived from the Latin *sedes*, meaning "seat."

CATHEDRAL
A cathedral contains the bishop's seat or throne, and is run by the dean and chapter. The chapter typically includes a chancellor, precentor (leads the congregation in singing), pastor, archdeacon, treasurer, canons (clergy members who are part of the chapter), and a clerk. The term *chapter* is derived from the sixth-century Rule of Saint Benedict, which included a directive that monks should gather daily for the reading of a chapter of the Bible.

ARCHDEACONRY
A smaller area within a diocese, under the authority of an archdeacon.

DEANERY
A group of parishes within a diocese, under the care of a rural dean (as distinct from a cathedral dean).

PARISH

The smallest division, under a vicar or, historically, a rector, dating from an age where tithes were payable to the incumbent.

ECCLESIASTICAL COURTS

Prior to the late 1850s, when national courts were established, many legal matters were administered through a hierarchy of ecclesiastical courts, similar to the secular courts of today, but with more interesting—and even peculiar—names.

Royal Peculiar (with courts)

A "peculiar" is a church that is outside the jurisdiction of the diocese in which it is located, and most are "royal"—they owe their allegiance directly to the sovereign. Westminster Abbey (where all British monarchs have been crowned since 1066) is an example of a royal peculiar.

Prerogative Court

The provincial court of the archbishops of Canterbury and York—effectively the Supreme Court of the Church.

Consistory Court

The court of a bishop. Consistory courts were established shortly after the Norman Conquest in 1066 and dealt with cases of defamation, probate, and matrimony as well as Church-related matters.

Archdeaconry Court

The court of an archdeacon. Until minor criminal jurisdiction passed to justices of the peace in the eighteenth century, it was the responsibility of the archdeaconry court.

Decanal Court

The court of a dean. The word *decanal* is derived from the Latin *decanus*, meaning "chief of a group of ten" (in this case, the chapter).

Peculiar Court

Again, a nonroyal peculiar is outside the jurisdiction of the diocese in which it is located, but in this case it is related, for example, to the chapel of a school, university, or the Inns of Court in London.

FIRST AMONG EQUALS

The Archbishops of Canterbury and York originally had equal status, but in 1071 the pope declared that Canterbury should take precedence. This was eventually formalized by an Act of Parliament in the reign of Henry VIII, and today the archbishop of Canterbury is recognized as *primus inter pares*—"first among equals."

THE CHURCH OF JESUS CHRIST OF LATTER-DAY SAINTS

The Church (aka LDS) was founded in 1830 with the publication of the *Book of Mormon*, which adherents believe is an English translation of a sacred Hebrew text relating the story of Israelite peoples who lived in America in ancient times. The existence of the text, said to have been lost for 1,500 years, was revealed by the Angel Moroni to Joseph Smith, who organized the LDS with a small group of believers. After Smith was murdered by an anti-Mormon mob, his successor, Brigham Young, led an exodus to Utah and established the Mormon settlement of Salt Lake City.

The Church, whose members are known as Mormons, is overseen by fifteen apostles, considered the "special witnesses" of Jesus Christ. There are also local congregations with their own hierarchy.

CHURCH LEADERS

First Presidency
The Church's highest governing body. It consists of the president, the most senior apostle, considered God's spokesman on Earth, and two counselors chosen by the president. The First Presidency of the Early Church comprised the apostles Peter, James, and John, selected by Christ.

Quorum of the Twelve
These apostles are the second-highest governing body. Traditionally, the original apostles number twelve in total, but the LDS interpretation of the New Testament has isolated the First Presidency, making the total fifteen.

Seventies
The Quorum of the Twelve is assisted by a third level of leaders called "seventies," who serve in various locations worldwide. They are so named because each group has up to seventy members, a reference to the seventy disciples of Christ mentioned in the Gospel of Luke. The Seventies are further divided into the Seven Presidents, the First Quorum, and the Second Quorum.

THE STAKE
The term *stake* derives from the Old Testament, referring to the stakes that supported the tabernacle, or tent— effectively a church, albeit a mobile one, and symbolically "the Church."

LOCAL CONGREGATIONS

Stake President
Local congregations are made up of administrative parishes called wards. A group of wards forms a stake, headed by the stake president, an unsalaried position. A stake president serves for about nine years.

Bishop
The leader of a ward, a bishop serves for about five years. This post is also unsalaried.

Members
The members of the Church themselves assist the local leaders in the administration of the wards.

THE ANGEL MORONI

Most Mormon temples display a statue of the Angel Moroni. They are all replicas of one of six versions of the statue; the first official Moroni, sculpted for the Salt Lake Temple, was covered in 22-karat gold leaf. Moronis located on top of a temple usually face east, and all hold a trumpet in the right hand, symbolizing spreading the gospel and the Second Coming of Jesus Christ.

SHINTO

Derived from the Chinese *shéndào*, meaning "the way of the gods," Shinto is a Japanese religion combining worship of ancestors and nature spirits with a belief in sacred power (*kami*) in all things, animate and inanimate. Visiting shrines is an important aspect of Shinto, and since 1946, when the emperor, also the high priest of Shinto, lost his divine status in Japan's Allied occupation following World War II, the shrine priesthood (*shinshoku*), traditionally hereditary, has become a profession requiring an advanced level of study. The hierarchy of qualifications, from lowest to highest, is:

CHOKKAI (UPRIGHTNESS)
The beginners' rank—entry level.

GONSEIKAI
Gonseikai priests are qualified to serve at village or township shrines. Candidates for this rank must display knowledge of Shinto shrines and ritual, including old customs, as well as Japanese history, ethics, literature, the *Kojiki* ("Record of Ancient Matters") and invocational prayers (*norito*).

SEIKAI (RIGHTEOUSNESS)
The qualification required to serve as head priest at prefecture-level

shrines or as a lower-ranked priest (*Negi*) at shrines nationwide. To achieve this rank, candidates must expand the knowledge required for the rank of Gonseikai to include shrine etiquette, philosophy, psychology, world religions, and the *Nihon Shoki* ("The Chronicles of Japan").

MEIKAI (BRIGHTNESS)

The qualification required to serve as head priest (*Guji*) or assistant priest (*Gonguji*) at shrines nationwide. Candidates must expand the knowledge required for the rank of Seikai to include the regulations contained in the *Engi Shiki* ("Institutes of the Engi Period"), Shinto documents, ancient rules and traditions, as well as history of religion (including Buddhism and Christianity) and world history. They must also perform a ritual.

JOKAI (PURITY)

The highest rank, awarded to those who have carried out many years' study of Shinto practice. It is achieved through recommendation rather than passing a test of knowledge.

IMPERIAL DIVINITY

The spiritual status of the emperor of Japan as descendant of the sun goddess Amaterasu became official doctrine around the eighth century AD, and even in modern-day Japan the Grand Shrine and subshrines of Ise, devoted to Amaterasu, play a key role in Shintoism. The high priest and priestess of the Grand Shrine of Ise are usually members or descendants of the imperial family.

STATE SHINTO

State Shinto, with the emperor and the ceremonies of the imperial household at its heart, was established in 1868 in the Meiji era. It was the official state religion until 1946, when an imperial rescript was issued in which Emperor Hirohito declared that he was not a living god.

SUMO

In Japanese sumo, wrestlers, or *rikishi*, use their weight, bulk, and strength to force their opponent out of a 4.6m- /15ft-diameter ring, or to put any part of their body on the ground other than the soles of their feet. Around 550 *rikishi* of various ranks compete in six divisions at any given time. The wrestlers move up and down the rankings depending on their performance in preceding tournaments, except for the highly respected *yokozuna* at the very top of the hierarchy. *Rikishi* are ranked numerically in descending order and are divided into east (most prestigious) and west groups, so the top rank in, say, *sandanme* is *sandanme* 1 east, and the second rank *sandanme* 1 west, followed by the third rank *sandanme* 2 east, and so on.

THE DIVISIONS

The number of wrestlers competing in each division is limited. Each wrestler belongs to a stable (*heya*) of three to twenty *rikishi* of different ranks. The lower-ranking wrestlers train and live at the stable full-time.

Makuuchi
The top division
Forty-two *rikishi*

Jūryō
Twenty-eight *rikishi*

Makushita
One hundred twenty *rikishi*

Sandanme
Around two hundred *rikishi*

Jonidan
Around 250 *rikishi*

Jonokuchi
Around eighty *rikishi*

Yokozuna (grand champion)
Excelling in skill, strength, and, importantly, also in dignity and grace, only just over seventy *rikishi* have achieved this rank to date since 1630, and there have been periods when no wrestlers at all have qualified to compete at this level. Unlike the rest of the ranks, *yokozuna* cannot be demoted but are expected to retire when they can no longer perform at their peak, even during a tournament (*honbasho*).

Ōzeki
A wrestler is considered for promotion (discretionary) to *ōzeki* if he wins thirty-three bouts over three consecutive tournaments. Perks include acting as dewsweeper or swordbearer for a *yokozuna*'s ring-entering ceremony and having junior wrestlers as personal attendants. The *banzuke* (official list of the rankings) requires there to be a minimum of two *ōzeki* at any one time, one east and one west.

Sekiwake
A wrestler needs a good record of wins in previous tournaments to be promoted to *sekiwake* and for there to be space available at that rank. There should be a minimum of two *sekiwake* at any one time (east and west).

Komusubi
To achieve this rank, *rikishi* must have achieved more wins than defeats in a tournament. There should be a minimum of two *komusubi* at any one time (east and west).

Maegashira
The remaining *rikishi* in the Makuuchi division, usually around thirty-two in total (sixteen east, sixteen west), depending on their performances at their previous tournament.

SEKITORI

Wrestlers in the top two divisions (*makuuchi* and *jūryō*) are also known as *sekitori*. They wear their hair in an *ōichō* (topknot fanned out into the shape of a ginkgo leaf, styled by specialist hair-dressers), wear colorful *mawashi* (belts), and can take part in ring-entering ceremonies. They are assigned lower-ranked wrestlers as personal attendants who are expected to wash their underwear, clean their rooms, serve their meals, run errands, etc. *Sekitori* are also allowed to get married and live away from the stable.

JUDO

Dr. Jigorō Kanō of Japan, founder of modern judo, came up with the colored belt system to indicate the progress of students or *judoka*, and the first black belts were awarded in the 1880s. This system became the basis for modern martial arts. *Judoka* usually start with a white belt, and the colors gradually become darker as skill and knowledge increase. Colors and standards can vary quite widely according to country, but western judo usually follows the order below, with six student grades, or *kyu*, leading up to the coveted black belt when a *judoka* becomes a *dan*, or advanced grade holder. The belt colors of the twelve advanced *dan* levels are more consistent across clubs and countries.

Judo places great emphasis on self-discipline and respect for others, and lower ranks are expected to show respect to *judoka* of more senior rank. Skill in practice and contest along with technical knowledge are required to advance to 5th *dan*, after which advancement for the *yudansha* ("person who has *dan*") is based on service to the sport.

6th kyu white
5th kyu yellow
4th kyu orange
3rd kyu green
2nd kyu blue
1st kyu brown
1st to 5th dan black
6th to 8th dan red-and-white
9th to 11th dan red
12th dan wider version
   of the white belt

KARATE

Gichin Funakoshi, a friend of judo founder Dr. Kanō, adopted judo's belt system and other fundamental characteristics for karate. Known as the grandfather of Japanese karate, he founded Shotokan, one of the most popular styles of karate today. Different styles of karate have different belt colors but generally begin with a white belt. A black belt is issued when a *karateka* (student of karate) has achieved a level of training and expertise that means they can then teach. The student ranking system includes ten *kyus—kyu* means grades away from the black belt or *dan*.

SHOKOTAN KARATE KYU BELTS (LOWEST TO HIGHEST)	DAN LEVEL (HIGHEST TO LOWEST, ALL BLACK BELT)
10th Jik-kyu white	10th Jyu-dan
9th Kyo-kyu orange	9th Ky-dan
8th Hachi-kyu red	8th Hachi-dan
7th Schichi-kyu yellow	7th Schichi-dan
6th Rok-kyu green	6th Roku-dan
5th Go-kyu purple	5th Go-dan
4th Yon-kyu purple/white	4th Yon-dan
3rd San-kyu second purple	3rd San-dan
2nd Ni-kyu first brown	2nd Ni-dan
1st Ik-kyu second brown, third brown/white, or black	1st Sho-dan

There are ten levels of black belt or *dan*, and each level takes longer than the last to achieve. The first few *dan* grades are awarded on physical ability, but higher levels are based on teaching experience, leadership, tenure, and service to the organization. Vladimir Putin was awarded the 8th dan in 2012, the first Russian to achieve this.

BELT UP

The *obi*, or belt, is worn around the waist as an indicator of the level of experience and training, and for practical purposes, keeping the jacket, or *uwagi*, closed and providing some protection for the vital organs. Traditionally *gis* (karate uniforms) were white, but students today may wear a colored uniform (e.g., red, blue).

THE JEDI ORDER

The Jedi (founded c. 25,000 BBY—Before the Battle of Yavin) are adherents of the Force, a network of energy that connects all living things in the galaxy. They are members of an ancient monastic organization that aims to promote peace and provide support to the weak, while continuing study of the Force.

JEDI INITIATE OR YOUNGLING

A child who is "Force-sensitive." Younglings are frequently sent away from the parental home to the Jedi Academy at a young age (varies according to species, four or five years for humans). There they are instructed by Jedi Masters, learning simple basic control over the Force and self-defense techniques.

PADAWAN

Jedi Knights or Masters choose a youngling to become their pupil. Younglings not chosen for special instruction may enter the Jedi Service Corps to specialize in, say, agriculture or exploration. Before being allowed to take the initiate Trials to Knighthood, padawans must construct their own light sabers.

KNIGHT

A padawan who has successfully completed the Trials, including the Trial of Flesh, the Trial of Courage, the Trial of Skill, the Trial of Spirit, and the Trial of Insight.

MASTER

A Jedi Knight who has performed a deed deemed extraordinary or exceptional in some way, or who has trained a padawan to be eligible for promotion to the rank of Knight.

GRAND MASTER

The head of the order and leader of the Jedi governing the body, the High Council. A very experienced Jedi Master, particularly noted for their wisdom, and often the most senior Jedi Master. They guide the Order and oversee its activities.

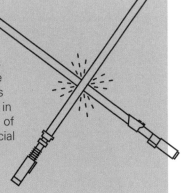

TO THE CAVES OF ILUM MUST YOU GO

As part of the Jedi tradition, initiates taking part in the ritual known as the Gathering travel to the Crystal Caves of Ilum to find a kyber crystal that is in tune with their individual awareness of the Force. The kyber crystal is a crucial component, being the source of the light saber's power.

STARFLEET

Starfleet's deep-space exploration really took off with the development of the first warp five–speed craft (*Enterprise* NX-01) in the 2150s, and continued after the founding of the United Federation of Planets in 2161. As a result, Starfleet's officers frequently assume the role of ambassador, often representing the first contact a civilization has with the Federation. The organization also takes on diplomatic (escorting dignitaries) and humanitarian (no matter what species) functions, as well as playing a defensive role. Starfleet's officer ranks are based on the naval ranks used on Earth. Cadets normally spend four years at Starfleet Academy in San Francisco, Earth, before graduating in one of three divisions: command (starships, starbases, Starfleet HQ), operations (operational departments of a starship, e.g., engineering), or science (research and medical). Promotion is strictly on the basis of merit.

At least one officer of distinction in Starfleet's long history is listed for each of the senior ranks given on page 70, although a number of them went on to reach a higher rank than the one listed. All those listed served in the twenty-third or twenty-fourth centuries:

FLAG OFFICERS

Commander in Chief
Top-ranking Fleet Admiral, commands the entire Starfleet—C. in C. Bill

Fleet Admiral
Harry Morrow

Admiral
Charlie Whatley

Vice Admiral
Kathryn Janeway

Rear Admiral
Erik Pressman

Commodore
Robert Wesley, USS *Lexington*

OFFICERS

Fleet Captain
Christopher Pike

Captain
Jean-Luc Picard, James Tiberius Kirk
of the USS *Enterprise* (NCC-1701)

Commander
William T. Riker

**Lieutenant Commander
(usually a departmental head)**
Montgomery Scott, Geordi La
Forge (engineering); Leonard
McCoy (medicine); Spock (science)

Lieutenant
Nyota Uhura (communications);
Hikaru Sulu (navigation)

Lieutenant Junior Grade
Dr. Julian Bashir; Worf (Klingon)

Ensign
Pavel Chekov; Harry Kim

JUNIOR OFFICERS AND CREWMEN

Master Chief Petty Officer
Senior Chief Petty Officer
Chief Petty Officer
Petty Officer First Class
Petty Officer Second Class
Crewman First Class
Crewman Second Class
Crewman Third Class

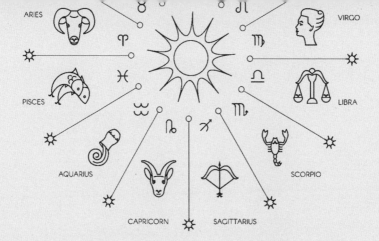

THE ZODIACAL CONSTELLATIONS

Constellations are the human imposition of patterns on the heavens; the stars in a constellation are rarely grouped together physically, and many are light-years apart. There are eighty-eight constellations altogether, of which the oldest established are the twelve zodiac constellations visible to everybody on Earth the whole year round. They occupy a narrow but busy band of sky, the ecliptic, which is the apparent path of the Sun as it rolls round the year, and the orbital plane of the Moon and the visible planets (Mercury, Venus, Mars, Jupiter, Saturn). The constellations provide a useful coordinate system to locate the Sun and the planets as they appear to pass in front of them.

The modern order of the astronomical zodiac was established by the Hellenic scholar Ptolemy (AD 90–168) some two thousand years ago, starting with Aries, which marked the position of the Sun at the spring equinox in the northern hemisphere. The chart shows the astronomical zodiac constellations in order of size. In order of sequence, both astrologically and astronomically, the zodiac starts with Aries and ends with Pisces, as listed.

CELESTIAL BESTIARY

These twelve constellations are known as the zodiac, from the Greek word *zoidion*, meaning "little animal," as most of them are imagined as real or mythical beasts.

ZODIACAL CONSTELLATION SEQUENCE

ARIES

TAURUS

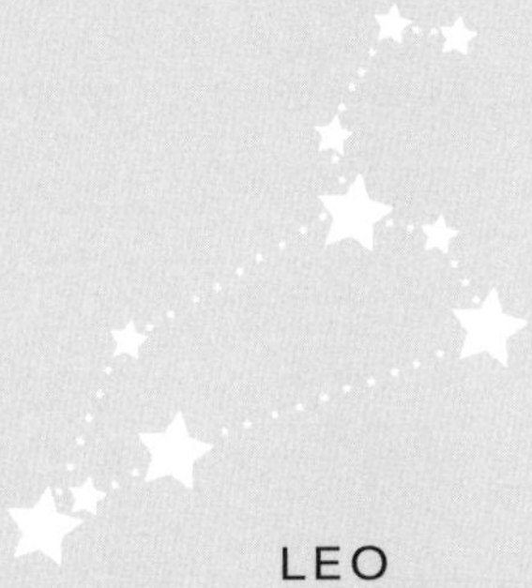

LEO

VIRGO

SCORPIO

CAPRICORN

AQUARIUS

GEMINI

CANCER

LIBRA

SAGITTARIUS

PISCES

BY SIZE

VIRGO 3.1 percent of sky
Brightest star: Spica

AQUARIUS 2.4 percent of sky
Brightest star: Sadalsuud

LEO 2.3 percent of sky
Brightest star: Regulus

PISCES 2.2 percent of sky
Brightest star: Alpherg or
Kullut Nunu

SAGITTARIUS 2.1 percent of sky
Brightest star: Kaus Australis

TAURUS 1.9 percent of sky
Brightest star: Aldebaran

LIBRA 1.3 percent of sky
Brightest star:
Zubeneschamali

GEMINI 1.2 percent of sky
Brightest star: Pollux

CANCER 1.2 percent of sky
Brightest star: Altarf

SCORPIO 1.2 percent of sky
Brightest star: Antares

ARIES 1.1 percent of sky
Brightest star: Hamal

CAPRICORN 1.0 percent of sky
Brightest star: Deneb Algedi

NASA ASTRONAUTS

Named after the Greek term meaning "space sailor," astronauts are men and women who boldly go into space, in this case for America's National Aeronautics and Space Administration. Their missions have varied over the years, but with the ending of the space shuttle program in 2011 and until a mission to Mars becomes more of a reality, astronauts currently aspire to join the International Space Station (ISS) orbiting Earth. It is an egalitarian profession—there is no room for egos and pulling rank in the close confines of the ISS, where astronauts live and work cheek by jowl for a minimum of six months at a time. The hierarchy, such as it is, is therefore based on experience.

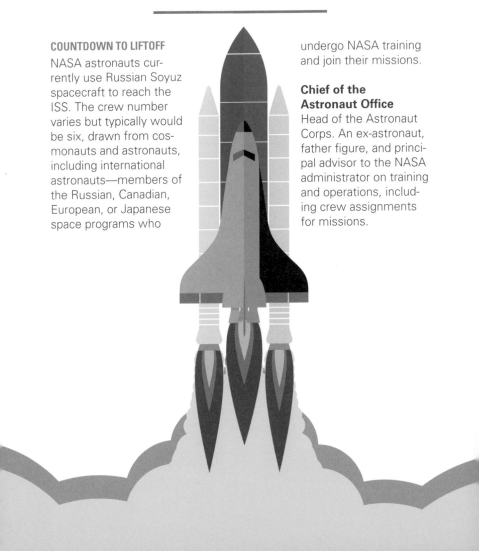

COUNTDOWN TO LIFTOFF
NASA astronauts currently use Russian Soyuz spacecraft to reach the ISS. The crew number varies but typically would be six, drawn from cosmonauts and astronauts, including international astronauts—members of the Russian, Canadian, European, or Japanese space programs who undergo NASA training and join their missions.

Chief of the Astronaut Office
Head of the Astronaut Corps. An ex-astronaut, father figure, and principal advisor to the NASA administrator on training and operations, including crew assignments for missions.

Commander

A highly experienced astronaut in overall charge of a mission, responsible for the crew's safety, the spacecraft, and making sure that the science on board is carried out properly and to schedule.

Pilot

Assists the commander. May also have other roles, such as undertaking EVAs (extravehicular activities—space walks).

Mission specialist

Specialist in and responsible for an aspect of a mission, for example, the onboard systems, payloads, usage of consumables, and education. They may also perform EVAs.

Astronaut candidate

Candidates must be U.S. citizens from the military or they may be civilians, but they must have a bachelor's degree in engineering, math, or physical, biological, or computer science, and be fit enough to pass the physical. Very few of the thousands of applicants are actually accepted. After having completed their training, and having taken part in a space flight more than 100 kilometers (62 miles) above Earth, new astronauts receive an astronaut pin (badge). Each service (Army, Navy, Air Force) issues their own pins featuring the astronaut device (a shooting star through a halo). Civilian astronauts receive special pins. The roles they take on as astronauts depend on their pre-NASA backgrounds, with engineers becoming mission specialists, pilots becoming commanders, and so on.

EXTRAVEHICULAR ACTIVITY (EVA)

Tech talk for the far more exciting (or terrifying) sounding layman's term *space walk*. It applies to any occasion on which an astronaut goes outside the craft when in space. Tethers attached to the spacecraft stop them floating off into the void, while a SAFER (Simplifed Aid for EVA Rescue) is a backpack that packs a jet-propelled punch to push the astronaut back to the craft in case of accidental untethering.

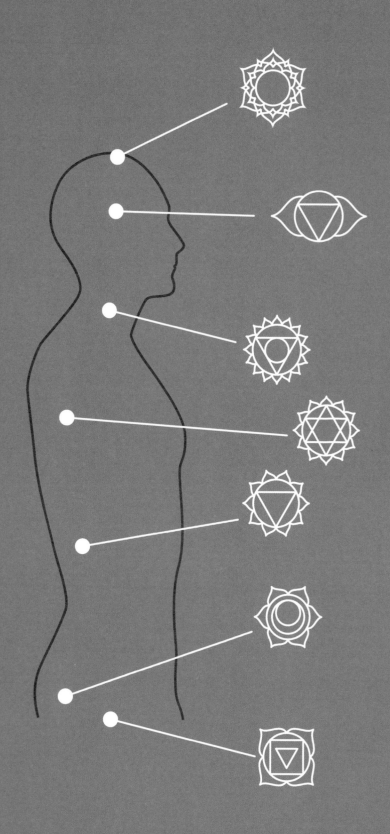

CHAKRAS

Chakra is a Sanskrit word for a spinning "wheel" of invisible energy or life force, called *prana*. There are seven main chakras, and according to Ayurvedic tradition they must remain open and aligned in order for the mind, body, and soul to be healthy and in harmony. It's akin to spinning plates on poles—let one fall, and they all go awry.

The bottom three chakras are related to the physical self and the top three to the higher, or spiritual, self. The heart chakra forms a bridge between the two aspects. The chakra hierarchy appears reversed, with the first chakra at the base of the spine and the seventh—the chakra of enlightenment, the state to which followers of Eastern spiritual traditions ultimately aspire—at the crown of the head.

MULADHARA
The first (root) chakra is at the base of the spine. It's associated with the color red and relates to material stability and security.

SVADHISTHANA
The second (sacral) chakra sits below the navel. It's associated with the color orange and relates to creative expression.

MANIPURA
The third (solar plexus) chakra lies between the navel and the breastbone. It's associated with the color yellow and relates to personal power.

ANAHATA
The fourth (heart) chakra is located in the center of the chest. It's associated with the color green and is the source of love and connection.

VISHUDDHA
The fifth (throat) chakra is in the neck area. It's associated with the color blue and relates to verbal expression.

AJNA
The sixth (third-eye) chakra sits between the eyebrows. It's associated with the color indigo and is the center of intuition, or sixth sense.

SAHASWARA
The seventh (crown, or "thousand petal lotus") chakra is located at the top of the head and thus is the only one not centered on the spinal column. It's associated with the color violet and is the chakra of enlightenment and spiritual connection to the Divine.

ICE AGES

In Earth's history, an ice age is defined as a long-term reduction of the temperature of Earth's surface during which the polar caps expand. This change in global climate can be caused by a variety of forces, including variations in Earth's orbit, the energy output of the Sun, plate-tectonic movement, levels of greenhouse gasses, ocean currents, and volcanic activity.

Scientists have studied the geological, chemical, and paleontological evidence and determined that Earth has experienced at least five major ice ages, beginning when ice covered the entire planet until today, when greenhouse gases have warmed the planet to the highest recorded temperatures.

ICE AGE: HURONIAN

Occurred: 2.4–2.1 billion years ago

Lasted: Approximately 300 million years

Life on Earth: Unicellular life-forms

ICE AGE: CRYOGENIAN

Occurred: 850 million years ago

Lasted: Approximately 200 million years

Life on Earth: Multicellular organisms

ICE AGE: ANDEAN-SAHARAN

Occurred: 460 million years ago

Lasted: Approximately 30 million years

Life on Earth: Trilobites, brachiopods, and cephalopods, all made extinct by the ice age

ICE AGE: KAROO

Occurred: 360 million years ago

Lasted: Approximately 100 million years

Life on Earth: Both fauna and flora, which was so abundant it was thought to have consumed most of the carbon dioxide in the atmosphere, triggering the ice age

ICE AGE: QUATENARY

Occurred: 2.6 million years ago

Lasts: Present day

Life: Humans, fauna, and flora

EARTH'S CORE TO THE TOP OF THE ATMOSPHERE

What comes first, the mantle or the outer crust? Is the mesosphere above the thermosphere? To help you keep track, following is a listing of layers from Earth's molten core to the edge of outer space.

INNER CORE
The most central layer on Earth, the inner core is 1,500 miles wide in diameter and composed mostly of iron that reaches scalding temperatures of around 10,800°F.

OUTER CORE
The outer core is a 1,400-mile-thick layer of liquid iron, sulfur, and nickel that ranges in temperature between 7,200 and 9,000°F.

MANTLE
Earth's mantle is 1,800 miles thick, and ranges between 1,800 and 6,700°F. The mantle becomes rockier the deeper you go but it is so hot that the rock flows, like lava. Convection currents, or the motion from constant cooling and reheating, moves the tectonic plates on the mantle, which creates earthquakes and builds mountains.

OUTER CRUST
The crust, where humans reside, is only three to five miles thick under the ocean and twenty-five miles thick under the continents.

TROPOSPHERE

From Earth's surface extending up to nine miles high, this layer contains clouds, and thus the weather that affects Earth's surface.

STRATOSPHERE

The second layer, which extends twenty-two miles above the troposphere, contains the ozone layer, which absorbs the Sun's ultraviolet radiation and keeps Earth warm. At the top of the stratosphere, air is almost a thousand times thinner than at sea level.

MESOSPHERE

The mesosphere extends twenty-two miles above the stratosphere. The top of this layer, which is the coldest part of the atmosphere, has temperatures of −130 degrees F. Meteors burn up at this layer.

THERMOSPHERE

This layer, which begins fifty-three miles above Earth and extends 319 miles, is where space shuttles fly and where the International Space Station orbits. Technically, the thermosphere is a part of the atmosphere, but is also considered space.

IONOSPHERE

This layer of electrons and atoms between the thermosphere and space, which extends up to six hundred miles from Earth's surface and overlaps the mesosphere, thermosphere, and exosphere, reflects radio waves and is an important buffer between the Sun and Earth.

EXOSPHERE

The outermost layer of Earth's atmosphere, which can begin between 320 and 620 miles from the surface depending on solar activity, is hard to distinguish from outer space.

THE HUMAN BODY

The human body has six associated levels of structural organization: chemical, cellular, tissue, organ, organ system, and organismal. The first, and simplest, of these includes the tiniest building blocks of matter essential for maintaining life; the highest, the organismal level, is the sum total of all the structural levels in our bodies.

1 CHEMICAL LEVEL

Atoms: the smallest unit of matter, two or more of which combine to form a molecule.

Molecules: (e.g., water molecules, DNA, glucose) these can be simple or complex and are the chemical building blocks of life, which combine to form...

Organelles ("little organs"): specific structures that perform specific functions within the body.

2 CELLULAR LEVEL

Cells: molecules are organized into cells, the smallest units of living matter and the basic units of structure and function of life, each with a unique task in the body. Cells vary in size, shape, and function (muscle cells, nerve cells, blood cells).

3 TISSUE LEVEL

Tissues: groups of similar cells are organized into tissues to perform a function (e.g., epithelial, connective, muscle, and nervous tissues). Each tissue has a role in the body.

4 ORGAN LEVEL

Organs: groups of at least two types of tissue that perform a specific function (e.g., liver, stomach, heart, lungs, brain).

5 ORGAN SYSTEM LEVEL

Organ systems: groups of organs that work together to perform a common function. There are eleven organ systems in the body: integumentary, muscular, skeletal, nervous, endocrine, cardiovascular, lymphatic, respiratory, digestive, urinary, reproductive.

6 ORGANISMAL LEVEL

Organ system: the highest level of structural organization, it consists of organ systems working together to perform a common function of the body and to keep a stable internal environment. It is the sum total of all the structural levels.

STRONG AND STABLE

The maintenance of a constant, stable, and balanced internal environment is known as homeostasis ("stay the same"). An example of this is the control of the amount of sugar in the blood. Diabetes is a condition that results from the body's inability to regulate its blood glucose levels.

ECOLOGICAL HIERARCHY

Ecological hierarchy theory describes the relationship between biological organisms. Living things are organized into increasingly larger and complex groups. From the top down they are as follows:

BIOSPHERE
All areas where life exists, that is, most of the earth, including the atmosphere, a sum of all the ecosystems.

BIOME
A set of ecosystems sharing similar characteristics.

ECOSYSTEM
Living organisms and nonliving aspects of the environment such as air, water, light, etc.

COMMUNITY
All the populations (plants, animals, microorganisms) in a specific area.

POPULATION
Members of the same species living in the same area at the same time and interacting with each other.

INDIVIDUAL SPECIES (ORGANISM)
Basic living systems.

PLANKTON

Plankton are diverse organisms that live in water and occur in sizes ranging from a few microns to meters. They are found in oceans, seas, lakes, rivers, and ponds and are traditionally divided into the following size-based categories, with the prefix referring to a metric unit of measurement:

FEMTOPLANKTON (*femto* meaning "one quadrillionth")

- mostly marine viruses, less than 0.2 µm in size

PICOPLANKTON (*pico* meaning "one trillionth")

- bacteria, cyanobacteria, 0.2–2 µm

NANOPLANKTON (*nano* meaning "one billionth")

- flagellates, 2–20 µm

MICROPLANKTON (*micro* meaning "one millionth")

- diatoms and cillates, 20–200 µm

MESOPLANKTON

- zooplankton and copepods, 0.2–20 mm

MACROPLANKTON

- larvaceans, larval fishes, and other zooplankton, 20–200 mm

MEGAPLANKTON

- jellyfish, salps, and other zooplankton, greater than 200 mm

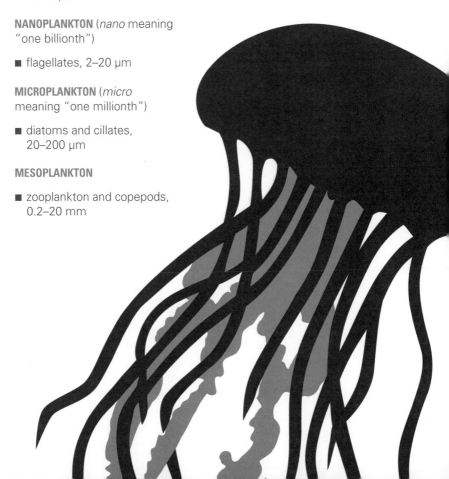

THE BODY MASS INDEX

Obesity has become a major problem in the developed world, contributing to a whole range of potentially life-threatening health issues. The Body Mass Index (BMI), a measure of body fat based on the ratio between a person's height and weight, is derived from the Quetelet Index, published in 1832 by Belgian statistician and sociologist Adolphe Quetelet.

Although Quetelet himself had no interest in obesity, the usefulness of his index as an indicator of the condition was identified 140 years later, and from 1995, when the term was adopted by the World Health Organization, BMI became the buzzword for flagging the point at which plump becomes perilous. And, of course, it works both ways—anything below the lower limit of the "normal" range is potentially dangerously underweight.

NORMAL
A BMI range of 18.5–24.9 is considered normal, and the range everyone should remain within to have the maximum chance of maintaining good health.

OVERWEIGHT
A range of 25–29.9 is a sign that it's time to adjust the diet, step up the exercise, and shed a few kilos.

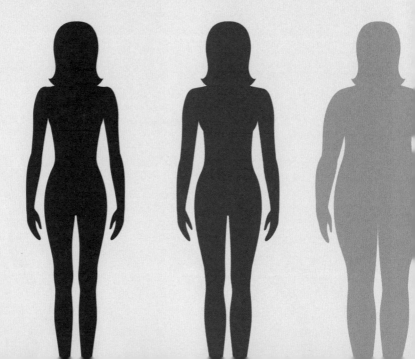

OBESE

The range 30–34.9 suggests you've tipped over into hazardous territory.

SEVERELY OBESE

A range of 35–39.9 means you're becoming ominously close to the peak of this hierarchy…

MORBIDLY OBESE

A BMI of 40 or above is considered literally life threatening. However, it is becoming increasingly apparent that BMI as an indicator of obesity as a health risk is not foolproof, partly because it assumes that everyone has exactly the same proportion of fat, muscle, and bone, but also because it does not take into account where in the body the fat is stored. There are two possibilities, and one is far more dangerous than the other:

BIG, MUSCLY INDIVIDUALS

Professional male rugby players are big, solid individuals, whose bulk is composed entirely of muscle—but based on the BMI, most would be classed overweight, if not clinically obese, highlighting the flaws in the system.

Subcutaneous obesity

This is where the fat is stored just under the skin. If you're going to store fat, hope for this low-risk type.

Visceral obesity

The fat is stored internally, particularly around the abdominal organs, and it's the high-risk type. A high waist-to-hip ratio is believed to be a telltale sign that this is where fat is lurking.

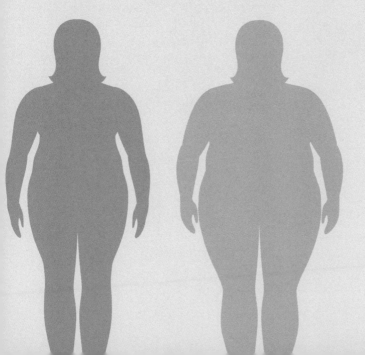

PERIODS OF SLEEP

Humans spend a third of their lives asleep, which is necessary for restoration of mind and body. Prior to the advent of modern medicine, most scientists believed that the brain was inactive during sleep. Through studying electrical patterns and eye movements, they now know that the brain goes through standard activity that comes in five periods. A person often cycles through these periods several times throughout the night.

STAGE 1

This is the five- to ten-minute period upon falling asleep when a person can be awakened easily. The eyes will move back and forth very slowly.

STAGE 2

Lasting 10–25 minutes, in stage 2 eye movements stop, body temperature lowers, and brain waves slow except for quick bursts of activity called sleep spindles.

STAGE 3

This stage, which last 20–40 minutes, produces delta waves, which are incredibly slow, and are interrupted by small, quicker waves. This is deep sleep with no eye or muscle movement.

REM

In REM sleep, which often happens 70–90 minutes after falling asleep, the breath quickens, the eyes scan quickly (which is why this stage is called Rapid Eye Movement), and the heart rate increases. Infants spend most of their sleep in REM. People often dream in this phase. During REM, the systems in the body are being repaired, including metabolism, the immune system, and the muscles.

HOW SWEET IT IS

Whichever way you look at it, excess sugar is bad for you. It can result not just in visits to the dentist but in weight gain and other health complications. Ranking the products that deliver sweetness in order of "least bad if you insist on having it" is not clear-cut, and the list (not exhaustive, starting with least bad) we offer here would be disputed by some experts. Most of the products are still high in sugar, so while some contain small amounts of minerals or nutrients (which you can also get from other food), it makes them only slightly "less bad" than sugar. And no matter how healthy nectar and honey may sound, they are still sugar, with all the accompanying health implications. Still, most people will perceive some benefit from replacing sugar with a "less bad" alternative, providing they don't use it as an excuse to add sugar to their diet.

The difference between the products here is really pretty minimal, and the advice is normally to limit sugar intake without avoiding it altogether.

Note: The list is not exhaustive—other sugars are available!

STEVIA

A natural sweetener produced as a powder or liquid from the leaves of the stevia plant. It is around two hundred times sweeter than sugar but is sugar free, contains no calories, and won't impact blood glucose levels. Counterintuitively, it leaves a slightly bitter aftertaste. As it is heat stable, it can be used in cooking as a sugar replacement.

XYLITOL

A sweetener that is found naturally in small amounts in fruit and vegetables but can also be produced artificially. It belongs to a group known as sugar alcohols, and although it contains some carbohydrate it contains fewer calories and has a lesser effect on blood sugar levels than sucrose. Studies indicate it has some benefits for dental health (it is often used in chewing gum and oral products). But don't overdo it; in quantity it can have a laxative effect.

HONEY

Raw honey contains some beneficial properties (antimicrobial and antibacterial). Regular honey is filtered and pasteurized to prevent it from crystallizing, but it loses some nutrients and vitamins in the process. Honey is sweeter than sugar and is still high in calories. Honey should not be given to infants, as it can cause infant botulism.

PURE MAPLE SYRUP (LIGHT TO DARK)

This contains some nutrients but is high in sugar. Don't confuse with maple-flavored corn syrup, which is usually higher in calories and lower in nutrients.

MOLASSES

A thick liquid produced after sugar is extracted from sugarcane. Several extractions are made; the first is lighter in color and contains more sugar, and so it is sweeter than the third, blackstrap molasses, although blackstrap contains more vitamins and minerals. But molasses is still high in sugar.

COCONUT SUGAR

From the sap of the coconut palm. The sap is extracted and then dried. It has some nutrient content but is about as high in calories as regular sugar.

RAW CANE SUGAR

From the sugarcane plant, it is less refined than white sugar... but it is still sugar and is high in calories.

GLUCOSE VS. FRUCTOSE

Glucose (aka dextrose) is found in many healthy foods. Virtually every cell in the body can metabolize glucose to give us energy, while the liver is the only organ that can metabolize significant amounts of fructose. Concerns have been raised that a higher intake of fructose has been linked to fatty liver disease, diabetes, cancer, and heart disease, although the research is far from being substantiated.

As artificial sweeteners (most are produced chemically) are much sweeter than sugar and contain no or fewer calories (but also no nutrients), they are often used to help control weight. Some are subject to investigation regarding side effects to health, and some studies are ongoing. Two examples: Aspartame (E951), 180 to 200 times sweeter than sugar. Questions have been raised about its potential effects on health, although many authorities have now found it safe. Those with the rare condition phenylketonuria (PKU) should, however, avoid it or get medical advice. Saccharin, around 300 times sweeter than sugar and often used in low-calorie food and drinks. Also investigated in the past for side effects on health, it is now permitted in processed food and drink at certain levels.

BROWN SUGAR (LIGHT TO DARK)

White sugar to which molasses has been added after the refining process. It contains a very small amount of nutrients but has the same number of calories as white sugar.

SUCROSE / TABLE SUGAR

From sugarcane or sugar beet. It is fifty-fifty glucose and fructose. Highly refined and processed as white sugar, it would be incorrect to say that it has no nutritional value whatsoever, as it does contain calories, and calories provide energy. But it is high in those calories and has no nutritional value beyond them.

CORN SYRUP / HIGH-FRUCTOSE CORN SYRUP (HFCS)

Produced from cornstarch and used in many foods, HFCS in particular has come in for criticism due to its high fructose content (see sidebar opposite). It has no nutritional value but delivers the same level of sweetness as sugar (contrary to popular belief) and is high in calories.

AGAVE NECTAR / SYRUP

Refined from the sap of the blue agave plant. It has a low GI (around 20) but is high in fructose (more than regular sugar), so when consumed in large amounts it may cause health problems (see sidebar opposite). All the beneficial properties of the plant are destroyed during the refining process.

THE SOLAR UV INDEX

Sunlight is an important source of vitamin D, made in the body when bare skin is exposed to sunlight; but exposing fair skin to sunlight can result in cancer. To help us take advantage of the former while avoiding the latter, the World Health Organization, the United Nations Environment Program, and the World Meteorological Organization collaborated to develop a UV Index (UVI), a measure of the level of harmful ultraviolet radiation, usually at its highest around solar noon.

The higher the number on the UVI, the greater the potential for skin and eyes to be damaged, and the faster that damage will occur. The numbers are represented by colors, ranging from "safe" green to "dangerous" violet, to provide instant recognition on weather charts showing forecast ultraviolet levels.

LOW

UVI 1 AND 2 (GREEN)
You can safely stay outside.

MODERATE

UVI 3, 4, AND 5 (YELLOW)

HIGH

UVI 6 AND 7 (ORANGE)
Seek shade during midday hours. Slip on a shirt,
slop on sunscreen, and slap on a hat.

VERY HIGH

UVI 8, 9, AND 10 (RED)

EXTREME

UVI 11+ (VIOLET)
Avoid being outside during midday hours. Make sure you seek
shade. Shirt, sunscreen, and hat are a must: Bright reflective
surfaces and white sand can double UV exposure.

ELEVATED UVI

On December 29, 2003,
a mind-blowing UVI
of 43 was recorded in
the Bolivian Andes of
South America. The high
elevation of the region,
combined with the mid-
day sun, is expected to
produce high levels, but
this measurement took
"extreme" to extremes.

THE BEAUFORT WIND FORCE SCALE

Developed in 1805 by British hydrographer Rear Admiral Sir Francis Beaufort, the scale is used to describe wind intensity on land and sea through observable conditions rather than precise measurements. Running from 0 (calm) to 12 (hurricane), it is the wind measurement scale most widely used today.

Beaufort Number	Wind speed (knots per hour)	Description
0	Less than 1	Calm
1	1–2	Light air
2	3–6	Light breeze
3	7–10	Gentle breeze
4	11–15	Moderate breeze
5	16–20	Fresh breeze
6	21–26	Strong breeze
7	27–33	High wind, moderate gale
8	34–40	Fresh gale
9	41–47	Strong gale
10	48–55	Whole gale/storm
11	56–63	Violent storm
12	64+	Hurricane

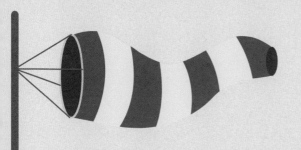

Wave height (in feet)	Sea	Land
0	Flat	Smoke rises vertically
0.33	Ripples	Wind moves smoke
0.66	Small wavelets that do not break	Wind can be felt on skin; leaves rustle
2	Large wavelets; some cresting	Leaves and smaller twigs in motion
3.3	Small waves	Dust and paper dance; small branches move
6.6	Moderate waves; some foam and spray	Moderate branches and small trees sway
9.9	Large waves, foaming crests, spray	Large branches sway; wind whistles through wires; trash cans fall over
13.1	Water heaps up, foaming streaks	Trees move; hard to walk against the wind; tall buildings sway
18	Moderate high waves, breaking crests, spray	Twigs break off trees; vehicles blown off course
23	High waves, dense foam	Larger branches and small trees break or blow over; damage to fences; tents blow down
29.5	Very high waves, large patches of boiling foam, much airborne spray	Trees broken off or uprooted; tiles blown off roofs
37.7	Exceptionally high waves, very large foam patches, airborne spray reducing visibility	Trees uprooted; roofs damaged or blown off
46+	Huge waves, entire sea white with foam, airborne spray reduces visibility to nothing.	Widespread damage to vegetation and structures; airborne debris

THE RICHTER SCALE

In 1935, Charles F. Richter of the California Institute of Technology developed his eponymous magnitude scale as a mathematical device for comparing the sizes of earthquakes. It used a formula based on the amplitude of the largest wave of energy as recorded by a seismograph, with adjustments made for the distance between the epicenter and the location of the various seismographs. The Richter scale has a base-10 logarithmic scale and is expressed in whole numbers with decimal fractions. Each whole number represents a tenfold increase in amplitude and the release of 31.7 times as much energy.

San Francisco's "Great Quake" in 1906 left almost 80 percent of the city damaged and was given a 7.8 rating. The largest quake ever recorded was a magnitude 9.5 in Chile on May 22, 1960. A 10 is thought to be impossible. The Richter scale does not provide accurate estimates for large-magnitude earthquakes and was succeeded in the 1970s by the moment magnitude scale (abbreviated as MW), which is preferred today; it measures an earthquake in terms of the energy released.

GREAT 8.0–8.9 AND 9.0 OR HIGHER

Felt across extremely large regions; severe damage to or total destruction of structures, including earthquake-resistant buildings. Honshu, Japan, 2011, 9.0.

MAJOR 7.0–7.9
Felt across great distances; collapse of / damage to many buildings within around 240 kilometers (150 miles) of the epicenter. Kathmandu, Nepal, 2015, 7.8.

STRONG 6.0–6.9
Felt up to hundreds of miles from the epicenter, strong/violent shaking in the epicenter; damage to well-constructed buildings, some damage to earthquake-resistant buildings. Northridge, California, 1994, 6.8.

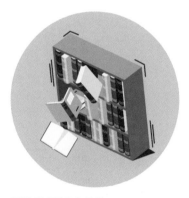

MODERATE 5.0–5.9
Possible slight damage to well-constructed buildings. Ontario–Quebec border, Canada, 2010, 5.0.

LIGHT 4.0–4.9
Noticeable shaking of indoor objects; usually only minimal damage.

MINOR 2.0–2.9 and 3.0–3.9
Felt by humans if they are near the epicenter; rarely causes damage.

MICROEARTHQUAKE 1.0–1.9
Barely felt by humans.

MOON PHASES

The Moon orbits around Earth every 29.5 days. During this lunar month, the Moon appears to change shape. These eight phases seen from Earth result from the angle the Moon makes with the Sun. For example, a full moon occurs when the Sun and Moon are at opposite sides of the sky, and the quarter stages are when the sun and moon are ninety degrees apart.

New Moon

Full Moon

Waxing Crescent

Waning Gibbous

First Quarter

Third Quarter

Waxing Gibbous

Waning Crescent

A blue moon occurs when there's an extra full moon within the year. A lunar eclipse is when Earth is positioned between the Moon and Sun, totally blocking the Sun's rays. These eclipses can be seen anywhere on the dark side of the earth.

THE SAFFIR-SIMPSON
HURRICANE WIND SCALE

A hurricane is defined as a storm with a violent wind, in particular a tropical cyclone in the Caribbean. To be classed as a hurricane, the wind speed must be force 12 on the Beaufort scale (see page 94)—that is, equal to or exceeding 119 kilometers (74 miles / 64 knots) per hour. People living in the hurricane belt have to be constantly on their toes, as the progression from a relatively innocent tropical depression to a "named storm" to a hurricane is often very rapid. The U.S. National Oceanic and Atmospheric Administration (NOAA) National Hurricane Center even organizes an annual "hurricane preparedness week" before the season starts, with daily tasks to be carried out, from "Determine your risk" to "Complete your written hurricane plan."

Developed in the 1970s by Herbert Saffir and Robert Simpson, the Saffir-Simpson Hurricane Wind Scale is based on a hurricane's sustained wind speed, defined as speed sustained for over one minute.

CATEGORY 1

Wind speed 119–153 km/h (74–95 mph; 64–82 kt/h)

Very dangerous; winds will produce some damage. Category 1 Hurricane Stan caused $3.96 billion worth of damage and 1,668 deaths in Mexico and Central America in 2005.

CATEGORY 2

Wind speed 154–177 km/h (96–110 mph; 83–95 kt/h)

Extremely dangerous; winds will cause extensive damage. The charmingly named but decidedly vicious Fife-Orlene caused $1.8 billion worth of damage and 8,000 deaths in Jamaica, Mexico, and Central America in 1974.

CATEGORY 3

Wind speed 178–208 km/h (111–129 mph; 96–112 kt/h)

Devastating damage will occur. The costliest (and third deadliest) U.S. hurricane, Katrina, was a mere category 3—but it still managed to inflict over $108 billion worth of damage to property, particularly in the New Orleans area. The exact death toll is uncertain, but figures between 1,200 and 1,836 were reported.

STORM DOD

The word *hurricane* comes from the Spanish *huracán*, thought to derive from the Taino god of storms, Hurakán. It was coined in the sixteenth century, when Spanish settlers were busy colonizing the Caribbean area.

**Wind speed 209–251 km/h
(130–156 mph; 113–136 kt/h)**

Catastrophic damage will occur. The storm with the highest death toll in the United States was the category 4 Great Galveston Hurricane of 1900, which caused an estimated loss of life of between 8,000 and 12,000. At this rating (and 5), most of the area will be uninhabitable for weeks or months.

NAME AND NUMBER

Storms (force 10 and 11 on the Beaufort scale) and hurricanes are given short, distinctive names for the purpose of unambiguous identification and communication when two or more storms are raging at the same time, often hundreds of miles apart. The system of using female names for storms began in 1953 and continued until 1978 (for the Northern Pacific) and 1979 (for the Atlantic basin), when male names were added. The list of names for Atlantic hurricanes is used on a six-year rotation, and a name is dropped only when it has been used for a storm particularly significant in terms of fatalities or cost.

**Wind speed 252 km/h
(157 mph/137 kt) or higher**

Catastrophic damage will occur. The record for the highest recorded wind speed at landfall is held by the 1969 category 5 Hurricane Camille, at an estimated 190 miles per hour when it struck the Mississippi coast.

HIGH CLOUDS (ABOVE 20.000 FEET)

CIRRUS
Appearance:
Thin, wispy, feathery clouds that don't produce precipitation

CIRROCUMULUS
Appearance:
Rows of fleecy clouds

MIDDLE CLOUDS

ALTOCUMULUS
Appearance:
Small, white, bunchy clouds made up of ice and water particles

LOW CLOUDS (BELOW 6,500 FEET)

CUMULONIMBUS
Appearance: Tall wide cloud stacks

Potential weather:
Thunderstorms with lightning

CUMULUS
Appearance: Fluffy white clouds

Potential weather:
Mild, occasional light showers

CLOUD CLASSIFICATIONS

Most clouds are formed as warm air rises in the atmosphere and the water vapor turns into tiny droplets of water or ice. Clouds are classified by their appearance and height above the earth. The clouds closer to the ground are primarily water particles, and those above twenty thousand feet are mostly composed of ice crystals.

CIRROSTRATUS
Appearance:
A thin, milky veil of ice crystals that signals an approaching weather front

(BETWEEN 6,500-20,000 FEET)

ALTOSTRATUS
Appearance:
Patchy, fluffy clouds thick enough to hide the sun or moon, which are usually a sign of rain.

NIMBOSTRATUS
Appearance:
Thick clouds that hide the sun and moon and produce rain or snow.

STRATUS
Appearance: Flat gray cloud cover

Potential weather:
Light drizzle

STRATOCUMULUS
Appearance: Clumps of puffy clouds with thin and thick areas

Potential weather:
Before or after a frontal system, possible drizzle

SEA STATES

The general state of the surface of a large body of water varies with the prevailing conditions. Determined by wave height, frequency, and power, it can be measured using instruments such as wave radar and weather buoys, or assessed visually by an experienced observer.

0 Calm (glassy)
0 meters (0 ft.)

1 Calm (rippled)
0 to 0.1 meters (0.00 to 0.33 ft.)

2 Smooth (wavelets)
0.1 to 0.5 meters (3.9 in. to

3 Slight
0.5 to 1.25 meters
(1 ft. 8 in. to 4 ft. 1 in.)

4 Moderate
1.25 to 2.5 meters
(4 ft. 1 in. to 8 ft. 2 in.

5 Rough
2.5 to 4 meters
(8 ft. 2 in. to 13 ft. 1 in.)

6 Very rough
4 to 6 meters (13 to 20 ft.)

7 High
6 to 9 meters (20 to 30 ft.)

8 Very high
9 to 14 meters (30 to 46 ft.)

9 Phenomenal
Over 14 meters (46 ft.)

ICEBERGS

Icebergs form when chunks of ice break away from glaciers or ice shelves—a process known as calving—in Arctic and Antarctic regions. Once calved, the iceberg drifts into more temperate waters and starts to erode and break up. Although it might be expected that the prosaically named "very large" category poses the biggest threat to shipping, it is in fact the smaller and more interestingly named bergy bits and growlers that are far more dangerous, as they are harder to spot. The most famous iceberg in history is the one the liner *Titanic* collided with on her maiden voyage in 1912. As a result, the International Ice Patrol (IIP), operated by the United States Coast Guard, was established the following year to keep North Atlantic shipping informed of potential danger and eliminate risk of collision. IIP categories are as follows:

VERY LARGE BERG
More than 75 meters (240 ft.) in height; more than 204 meters (670 ft.) in length.

LARGE BERG
46–75 meters (151–240 ft.) in height; 123–204 meters (401–670 ft.) in length.

MEDIUM BERG
16–45 meters (51–150 ft.) in height; 61–122 meters (201–400 ft.) in length.

SMALL BERG
5–15 meters (14–50 ft.) in height; 15–60 meters (47–200 ft.) in length.

A CUT ABOVE

The world's largest recorded iceberg, known as B-15, was nearly 300 kilometers (186 miles) long and 40 kilometers (25 miles) wide (that's a staggering 300,000 m / 982,080 ft. long and 37,000 m / 132,000 ft. wide), leaving no shred of doubt as to which category it fell into. It calved from the Ross Ice Shelf in Antarctica in March 2000; satellite imagery revealed that a fragment of the berg was still drifting thirteen years later.

BERGY BIT

1–4 meters (3–13 ft.) in height; 5–14 meters (15–46 ft.) in length.

GROWLER

Less than 1 meter (3 ft.) in height; less than 5 meters (16 ft.) in length.

AUSTRALIAN BUSHFIRES

Bushfires have been a part of the landscape in Australia for millions of years. They occur regularly in the hotter months in both mountainous and flat regions, in forested areas, grass, scrub or bush. The Australian FDR (Fire Danger Rating) was adopted by all the country's states in 2009 and is based on forecast weather conditions from the Bureau of Meteorology. Advice is given about the level of threat on a particular day. The fires usually occur during periods of high temperature, low humidity, and strong winds, and can be devastating. The Black Saturday bushfire of 2009 in Victoria destroyed more than two thousand homes, with 173 fatalities.

0–11 LOW TO MODERATE & 12–31 HIGH

Fires are likely to be controlled under these conditions and homes can provide safety. Bushfire survival plans should be checked.

32–49 VERY HIGH

Fires could be difficult to control by firefighters in these conditions, which are likely to be hot, dry, and possibly windy. Well-prepared and well-defended homes can provide safety, with vital equipment including a water supply, a gas/diesel portable pump, a generator, and protective clothing.

50–74 SEVERE & 75–99 EXTREME

In hot, dry, and windy conditions, fires that take hold move quickly, and are unpredictable and difficult for firefighters to bring under control. Spot fires are likely to start and spread quickly. Only homes with bushfire protection and active defenses may provide safety. Equipment required is the same as for the previous category, and fire risk areas should be left early in the day. The only safe place is away from bushfire risk areas.

100+ CATASTROPHIC

The worst conditions for bushfires. If a fire starts and takes hold, firefighters find it extremely difficult to control. Spot fires start ahead of the main fire and cause the fire to spread rapidly. The only safe place is away from bushfire risk areas. Immediate action is required.

NUCLEAR EVENT

The INES (International Nuclear and Radiological Event Scale) rates any event associated with the use, storage, and transport of radioactive material and radiation sources. Its purpose is to ensure that nuclear authorities, the public, and the media understand an event's "safety significance." Events are rated over seven levels; the severity increases approximately ten times with each increase in level, which looks at three categories of impact: people and the environment, radiological barriers and control (unplanned high radiation levels inside facilities), and defense-in-depth (protection measures that did not function as intended).

INCIDENT

LEVEL 1 ANOMALY
Overexposure of a member of the public in excess of the statutory annual limits; minor problems with safety components.

LEVEL 2 INCIDENT
Atucha, Argentina, 2005; Cadarache, France, 1993; Forsmark, Sweden, 2006
Significant contamination within a facility into an area not expected by design; exposure of workers in excess of the statutory annual limits, exposure of a member of the public in excess of 10 mSv (millisieverts—radiation is generally measured in sieverts, after the Swedish physicist Rolf Maximilian Sievert).

LEVEL 3 SERIOUS INCIDENT
Sellafield, UK, 2005; Vandellos, Spain, 1989
Exposure in excess of ten times the statutory annual limit for workers. Nonlethal health effect. Severe contamination in an area not expected by design, low probability of significant public exposure.

LEVEL 4 ACCIDENT WITH LOCAL CONSEQUENCES

Tokaimura, Japan, 1999; Saint Laurent des Eaux, France, 1980

Minor release of radioactive material, unlikely to require implementation of countermeasures other than food controls; at least one death from radiation. Release of significant quantities of radioactive material within an installation, significant public exposure highly likely.

LEVEL 5 ACCIDENT WITH WIDER CONSEQUENCES

Three-Mile Island, USA, 1979; Windscale Piles, UK, 1957

Limited release of radioactive material likely to require implementation of countermeasures; several deaths from radiation. Severe damage to reactor core; large quantities of radioactive

material released within an installation, significant public exposure highly likely.

LEVEL 6 SERIOUS ACCIDENT

Kyshtym, Russia, 1957

Significant release of radioactive material likely to require implementation of countermeasures.

LEVEL 7 MAJOR ACCIDENT

Chernobyl, Ukraine, 1986; Fukushima, Japan, 2011

Major release of radioactive material; widespread effects on health and the environment requiring implementation of planned and extended countermeasures.

Events with no safety significance are not rated.

Note: The above excludes the INES Defense-in-Depth rating except for Level 1.

DEFCON

This famous ranking system with its attention-grabbing alternative names describes the defense readiness of U.S. military forces to deal with a perceived threat to national security. It was first mapped out in 1959.

DEFCON 1 (COCKED PISTOL OR WHITE ALERT)

"Maximum Defense Readiness Condition"—nuclear war imminent. This level has never been implemented.

DEFCON 2 (FAST PACE OR RED ALERT)

The armed forces are ready to be deployed in six hours or less. This level was reached in the Cuban Missile Crisis in 1962.

DEFCON 3 (ROUND HOUSE OR YELLOW ALERT)

A state of military readiness.

DEFCON 4 (DOUBLE TAKE OR GREEN ALERT)

Security is strengthened and intel gathered.

DEFCON 5 (FADE OUT OR BLUE ALERT)

A state of peace, no immediate need to be on alert.

TERRORIST THREAT IN THE USA

The five-color alert system (from green to red) instigated in the United States by the George W. Bush administration in 2002 after the attacks of 9/11 was deemed too vague, scaring rather than preparing people for action. It was replaced in 2011 by a simple two-tier system devised by the National Terrorism Advisory System (NTAS). The alert is issued for a specific period only.

IMMINENT THREAT ALERT

A credible, specific, and impending terrorist threat against the United States.

ELEVATED THREAT ALERT

A credible terrorist threat against the United States.

DANTE'S CIRCLES OF HELL

According to the Italian poet Dante, who was given a tour of the place by Virgil, Hell consists of a vestibule followed by nine circles of suffering, subdivided by three rivers, boring deep into the underworld and centered on Satan, trapped in ice at the center of the earth. It is encircled by a Dark Wood patrolled by a lion, a leopard, and a she-wolf. The circles are concentric, each being reserved for a specific sin; the circles increase in wickedness as the center of the earth is approached, culminating in betrayal. The deeper it goes, the more complicated the architecture. Dante described it in detail in "The Inferno," a section of his long three-part narrative poem *The Divine Comedy*, completed in 1370 and published in 1432.

VESTIBULE
Sinners
The uncommitted, don't-knows, and opportunists.

Punishment
To run forever in fog, flowing with blood and pus and covered in maggots, and pursued by swarms of wasps and hornets.

River Acheron

FIRST CIRCLE
Limbo.

Sinners
The unbaptized, virtuous pagans; includes large numbers of classical poets and philosophers, and Virgil himself.

Punishment
Eternity spent in a castle representing an inferior form of heaven.

SECOND CIRCLE
Sinners
The lustful.

Punishment
Constantly buffeted by violent winds and terrible storms in pitch-black darkness.

THIRD CIRCLE
Sinners
The gluttons.

Punishment
Blinded and forced to wallow in icy, putrescent sludge and flayed by the claws of Cerberus if they try to get out.

FOURTH CIRCLE
Sinners
The greedy, misers, profligates, hoarders, and spendthrifts.

Punishment
Smothered in heavy weights and forced to fight by rolling over and crushing each other.

River Styx

FIFTH CIRCLE
Sinners
The angry.

Punishment
The Styx runs through this circle, forming the Stygian swamp. The enraged fight each other in the slime, while the passive-aggressive lie under the mud to putrefy.

The City of Dis, the entrance to Lower Hell. Guarded by fallen angels.

SIXTH CIRCLE
Sinners
Heretics.

Punishment
Crammed into burning tombs.

SEVENTH CIRCLE
This circle, the designated abode of the violent, is guarded by the Minotaur and is divided into three separate rings.

Ring One
Sinners
Those violent against their neighbors: warmongers, murderers, tyrants, and plunderers.

Punishment
Immersed in the Phlegethon, a river of boiling blood and fire; the more violent they were in life, the deeper they plunge. Armed centaurs patrol the banks and shoot anyone who tries to get out.

Ring Two
Sinners
Those violent against themselves; suicides.

Punishment
Transformed into gnarled trees in the Wood of Suicides, where they are pecked by Harpies.

Ring Three
Sinners
Those violent against art, nature, and God; blasphemers, sodomites, and usurers.

Punishment
Stranded on the burning hot sands of a great desert, tormented by flakes of fire that fall like rain. Blasphemers are forced to lie on their backs on the sand; sodomites are forced to run constantly in circles; usurers crouch and weep constantly.

The River Phlegethon forms a waterfall that leads down to the Eighth Circle.

EIGHTH CIRCLE
Malebolge
This circle is divided into ten concentric trenches (bolge) and is shaped like an amphitheater.

Trench One
Sinners
Panderers and seducers.

Punishment
March around the ditch continuously while being whipped by horned demons.

Trench Two
Sinners
Flatterers.

Punishment
Immersed in excrement.

Trench Three
Sinners
Simoniacs: people who sold ecclesiastical office and preferment.

Punishment
Rammed headfirst into narrow, font-like holes in the rock and burned on the soles of their feet.

Trench Four
Sinners
Magicians, diviners, astrologers, false prophets.

Punishment
Heads twisted 180 degrees and forced to walk backward.

Trench Five
Sinners
Corrupt politicians.

Punishment
Immersed in a lake of boiling pitch; tormented by Malebranche, demons with claws and grappling hooks, if they try to get out.

Trench Six
Sinners
Hypocrites.

Punishment
Forced to walk perpetually wearing lead-lined gilded robes.

Trench Seven
Sinners
Thieves.

Punishment
Trapped in a pit of biting reptiles, snakes, and lizards; repeatedly consumed by fire.

Trench Eight
Sinners
Counselors of fraud; people who advise others to be fraudulent; evil éminences grises.

Punishment
Constantly encased in flame.

Trench Nine
Sinners
Sowers of discord in the family, the community, or religious matters.

Punishment
Repeatedly hacked to pieces by a huge demon with a sword.

Trench Ten
Sinners
Falsifiers: alchemists, impostors, counterfeiters, liars.

Punishment
In constant darkness, afflicted with hideous diseases.

In the center of Malebolge is the well that leads down to the bottom-most Circle.

NINTH CIRCLE
At the bottom of this circle is Cocytus, the lake of ice, the abode of traitors. It is divided into four concentric lanes.

Lane 1 Caina
Sinners
Traitors to family and kindred.

Punishment
Frozen up to their necks in ice, but can move their heads.

Lane 2 Antenora
Sinners
Traitors to country.

Punishment
Frozen up to their chins in ice, but can move their heads.

Lane 3 Ptolomea
Sinners
Traitors to guests.

Punishment
Stretched out on their backs on the ice, their tears freezing their eyeballs.

Lane 4 Judecca
Sinners
Traitors to lords and benefactors.

Punishment
Their entire bodies immersed in the ice.

Satan is trapped up to his waist in the center of the lake. He has three faces and gnaws on a traitor in each mouth. Julius Caesar's assassins are being eternally consumed, Brutus on the left and Cassius on the right, while treacherous apostle Judas Iscariot is in the center.

TYPOGRAPHY

The way type is organized helps establish the importance of the information being presented. It guides the reader's eye, allowing them to navigate content easily, signaling the beginnings and ends of text and picking out important data. Typographic hierarchy is unusual in that the most important item in a document may not be positioned at the top and the hierarchy is fluid, changing according to the design of the document or text.

The tools most commonly used for typographic styling are listed below. They can be used in any combination by a skilled and creative graphic designer, but a conventional and fairly obvious hierarchy would be:

Size: The most obvious way of demonstrating importance.

Weight: Using a heavier (i.e., bolder/thicker) font.

Color: A useful way of picking out type. Warm colors (reds, oranges) generally shout out at us, while blues and greens recede more against a white background, for example.

Contrasting font: Different typefaces also add emphasis.

Position: Where type is positioned in a document also affects emphasis, drawing the eye.

Spacing: Type in isolation, for example, may stand out more.

LEVEL ONE
The most important content should be the most immediately visible. In a newspaper article, this could be a headline.

LEVEL TWO
The text should be organized into clear sections so the reader can easily navigate to the part they want. In a newspaper, a subheading.

LEVEL THREE
The substance of the document should be easy to read. In a newspaper, the text of the article.

TOLKIEN'S RINGS OF POWER

J. R. R. Tolkien's epic *The Lord of the Rings* (1953–1954) focuses on the quest to destroy the One Ring of Power and Sauron, its evil creator, but there are twenty rings in the story. Sauron, in disguise, helped to make sixteen of them with Celebrimbor the Elven smith, intending to give them to Dwarves and Men to keep them in his power. Celebrimbor alone made the three Elven rings. Sauron forged the One Ring that he thought ruled them all.

THE ONE RING

Gold. No stone. Elven script of an incantation in the Black Speech of Mordor, visible only when the ring is put in fire.

Powers: bends all others to its will; can make the wearer invisible and prolong their life.

Worn by: Sauron, Isildur, Gollum (Sméagol), Bilbo Baggins, Frodo Baggins, Sam Gamgee (briefly).

THE THREE ELVEN RINGS

VILYA

Gold with a blue stone/sapphire. Also known as the Ring of Air, the Ring of Firmament, and the Blue Ring.

Powers: healing, control of the elements.

Worn by: Elrond, Elf Lord of Rivendell.

NARYA

Gold with a red stone/ruby. Also known as Narya the Great, the Ring of Fire, the Red Ring, and the Kindler.

Powers: resistance to evil, inspiring hope in others.

Worn by: Gandalf the Wizard.

NENYA

Mithril (silver) with a white stone/diamond. Also known as the Ring of Water, the Ring of Adamant, and the White Ring.

Powers: protection and preservation from evil.

Worn by: Galadriel, Elf Queen of Lothlórien.

THE SEVEN RINGS

These rings have no individual names.

Powers: intensifies the dark side of the dwarf mind, leading to an obsession with amassing gold.

Worn by: the Chief of each of the dwarf clans: Longbeards (Durin's Folk), Firebeards, Broadbeams, Ironfists, Stiffbeards, Blacklocks, Stonefoots.

These rings all have equal power. Four were destroyed by dragons, and three were taken back under torture by Sauron.

THE NINE RINGS

These were made by Sauron for men who had already gone to the dark side. Only the Witch King of Angmar is named in Tolkien's work.

Powers: bends the wearer to the will of Sauron.

Worn by: the Nine Riders, also known as the Ring Wraiths and the Nazgûl.

All were destroyed when the One Ring was destroyed in the fires of Mount Doom.

HOUSES AT HOGWARTS

In J. K. Rowling's *Harry Potter* book and movie series, the sorting hat sits on every wizard's and witch's head to decide which house they belong to—Gryffindor, Hufflepuff, Ravenclaw, or Slytherin—which are named after the four founders of Hogwarts. Family members often remain in the same house. For example, Draco Malfoy's parents were also in Slytherin, while Harry Potter's parents were also in Gryffindor.

However, some Hogwarts students don't have wizard parents, and they are called "Muggles." They are often looked down upon as inferior, along with Squibs, who are children of wizards but who don't have any capacity for magic. Half-bloods are children who have one magical parent and one Muggle parent (Harry Potter's children will be half-bloods). Pure bloods have no Muggles within their family tree, like the Malfoy family, and they believe that makes them superior.

	Gryffindor
CHARACTERISTIC	Bravery
ANIMAL	Lion
COLORS	Scarlet and Gold
MEMBERS	Albus Dumbledore Harry Potter Ron Weasley Hermione Granger Rubeus Hagrid Sirius Black James and Lily Potter Dean Thomas

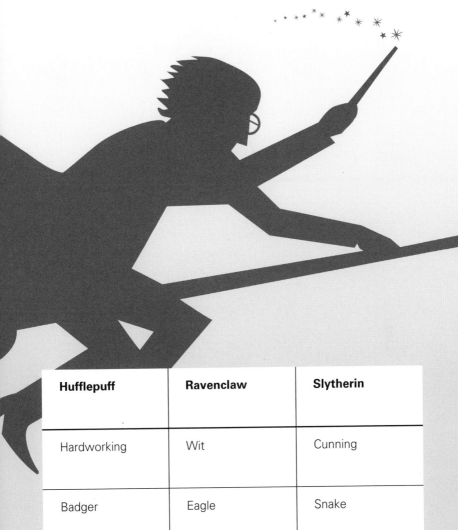

Hufflepuff	Ravenclaw	Slytherin
Hardworking	Wit	Cunning
Badger	Eagle	Snake
Yellow and Black	Blue and Bronze	Green and Silver
Cedric Diggory Nymphadora Tonks Hannah Abbott Cadwallader Justin Finch- Fletchley Zacharias Smith Pomona Sprout Eloise Midgeon	Cho Chang Luna Lovegood Filius Flitwick Padma Patil Roger Davies Gilderoy Lockhart The Grey Lady (Helena Ravenclaw) Garrick Ollivander	Bellatrix Lestrange Tom Riddle (Voldemort) Gregory Goyle Vincent Crabbe Regulus Black Severus Snape Horace Slughorn

COMMUNIST PARTY OF THE SOVIET UNION (CPSU)

The CPSU was created by members of the Bolshevik wing of the Russian Social Democratic Workers' Party (RSDWP) led by Vladimir Lenin after the Russian Revolution of October 1917. It held power until 1991 when the Soviet Union broke up under its last general secretary, Mikhail Gorbachev. At its peak, the CPSU had around nineteen million members.

Although in many people's minds the Communist Party and the Soviet government were one and the same thing, in practice they were two separate entities, and it was the CPSU that governed. The Party's structure paralleled that of government, so that at each level (province, district, city) the government official had an equivalent in the Party, but the Party official's status was superior, and most of the high-ranking government officials were also Party members.

PARTY CONGRESS

The CPSU's governing body, which initially met annually (subsequently less frequently) and was attended by several thousand delegates. It elected the members of the Central Committee, which governed between congresses. The Congress was the supreme power until the general secretary gradually took over the top spot—a change that began in 1922 when Joseph Stalin was elected general secretary and by the end of the decade had become virtual dictator.

CENTRAL AUDITING COMMISSION

Elected by and reported to the Party Congress, the Commission had a supervisory role, monitoring the handling of affairs by the Party's central bodies and the

Central Committee, and auditing the treasury's accounts.

CENTRAL COMMITTEE

With around three hundred members (by the 1980s), the Central Committee met twice a year and handled party administration as opposed to policy. It elected the members of the various committees, including the Politburo and the Secretariat, in theory, although in practice both elected their own members.

CENTRAL CONTROL COMMISSION

Elected by the Central Committee of which it was a part, the Commission supervised the discipline of Party members, handing out punishments and issuing expulsions.

GENERAL SECRETARY

Known as first secretary from 1952 to 1966. The general secretary was de facto head of the Politburo, from among whose members he was elected. Under Stalin it became the most powerful position in the Party and synonymous with, first, Party leader and, later, leader of the whole Soviet Union.

POLITBURO (POLITICAL BUREAU)

Known as the Presidium from 1952 to 1966, it had around fifteen full members. The highest policy-making body (both domestic and foreign), the Politburo eventually overshadowed the Central Committee. Although theoretically elected by the Central Committee, in reality the Politburo elected its own members, who for most of its existence included the minister of defense, the foreign minister, and the chairman of the KGB.

SECRETARIAT

The Secretariat oversaw the administration of the regional governments and the police, army, and KGB, and helped develop policy for the Politburo. Its different departments were headed by secretaries.

Below the Secretariat, the Party was organized, and wielded power, via a series of conferences and committees at republic (state), province (oblast), and district (raion) levels, right down to the smallest unit of all, the primary Party organization.

PRIMARY PARTY ORGANIZATION

Otherwise known as the Party cell. Any organization (farm, factory, school, and so on) that contained at least three Party members could form a Party cell.

YOUTHFUL ENTHUSIASM

Theoretically independent of the CPSU, the Komsomol prepared young people aged fourteen to twenty-eight for Party membership. Children aged nine to fourteen joined the Pioneer wing, while politically mature children below the age of nine joined the Little Octobrists. By the 1970s and 1980s membership had reached the forty million mark.

INTERNATIONAL DIPLOMACY

Diplomacy in some form has been oiling the waters of relations between clans, cities, and kingdoms since people first recognized the value of getting along with their neighbors instead of attacking them. In Europe, the roots of modern diplomacy are frequently traced back to the early Renaissance and the city-states of northern Italy. By the seventeenth century, French had replaced Latin as the lingua franca of diplomacy, and although itself now largely replaced by English, the influence of French is still much in evidence in many of the terms used. At the Congress of Vienna in 1815, when parts of Europe were "reorganized" after the Napoleonic Wars, four senior diplomatic ranks were recognized:

- **Ambassadors, legates, and nuncios**
- **Envoys and ministers**
- **Ministers resident**
- **Chargés d'affaires**

But in 1961 after the Vienna Convention on Diplomatic Relations, the rank of minister resident (a diplomatic agent resident at a foreign government) was dropped, leaving three ranks of head of mission (principal official of a diplomatic mission), in descending order:

AMBASSADORS OR NUNCIOS (PAPAL AMBASSADORS)
Accredited to the host country's head of state and other heads of mission of equivalent rank.

ENVOYS EXTRAORDINARY, MINISTERS PLENIPOTENTIARY (WITH "FULL POWERS"), AND INTERNUNCIOS (PAPAL ENVOYS) AND OTHER REPRESENTATIVES
Accredited to the host country's head of state.

CHARGÉS D'AFFAIRES (AD HOC)
Usually accredited to the host country's minister of foreign affairs, rather than to the head of state.

CHARGÉS D'AFFAIRES (AD INTERIM)
A diplomatic agent deputizing for an absent head of mission.

DIPLOMATIC CORRESPONDENCE
The correspondence between one state and another is highly stylized, using elaborate, established courtesy phrases. It takes the form of letters (e.g., letters of credence granting diplomatic accreditation, letters of recall—of an ambassador) or notes. Some of the most commonly used are listed below in descending order of formality and importance. However, diplomacy is not immune to

the recent rapid changes in communication technology, and many diplomats now also communicate by email, when they must use all their innate prudence and vigilance to guard against an overimpulsive click of the "send" button.

FIRST-PERSON NOTE

For the most important correspondence, such as between a head of mission and the head of a foreign ministry or a foreign diplomatic mission. Signed.

THIRD-PERSON NOTE

Written in the third person, so the first and second person pronouns (*I, we, you, your*) must not be used. With a few exceptions, not signed but initialed in the lower right corner of the last page. Third-person notes include:

NOTE VERBALE

As the name implies, a note verbal was originally a written record of information delivered orally. It begins with a courtesy phrase.

MEMORANDUM

A written statement on any, usually routine, subject. Courtesy phrases are used if it is custom.

AIDE-MÉMOIRE

An "aid to memory," a note summarizing the key points of an informal conversation or interview, without committing the issuing delegation's country to the contents. It does not begin with a courtesy phrase.

BOUT DE PAPIER

A "piece of paper," a very informal way of presenting written information.

OTHER NOTES

These include the **note diplomatique**, a formal note between governments, with courtesy phrases; **note collective**, addressed to or sent by two or more governments (little used due to the difficulty in getting all parties to agree on its wording); **circular diplomatic note**, an identical note from a single state to multiple states.

THE BRITISH ROYAL HOUSEHOLD

Since 1688, Britain has had a constitutional monarchy, whereby Parliament, not the sovereign, is the ruling power; virtually all countries with a monarchy now have the same system. However, with numerous State and public duties to perform, being king or queen is still a very demanding role, requiring a large support network. In Britain, each member of the royal family has its own household. The sovereign's household currently has three Great Officers—the Lord Chamberlain, who coordinates the five main departments that keep the royal machine running smoothly, and the Lord Steward and the Master of the Horse, whose roles are ceremonial.

THE PRIVATE SECRETARY'S OFFICE

This department supports the sovereign's work as head of State. The team's responsibilities include organizing official visits, both at home and abroad, and advising on constitutional matters.

THE PRIVY PURSE AND TREASURER'S OFFICE

Besides managing the royal finances, it covers practical aspects of running the family "firm," such as human resources and technology.

THE MASTER OF THE HOUSEHOLD'S DEPARTMENT

Masterminds both official and private entertaining and includes all those involved in hospitality, such as caterers and florists.

THE LORD CHAMBERLAIN'S OFFICE

Manages all the ceremonial events, from State visits and the State Opening of Parliament to royal weddings and garden parties, and is also responsible for travel.

ROYAL COLLECTION

Manages the care and presentation of the royal art collection, as well as the opening of the official royal residences to the public.

SPECIALIST HOUSEHOLDS

These include the ecclesiastical household, which includes clergy and organist/choirmaster/composer for the Chapels Royal, and the medical household, which covers every eventuality from surgery to dentistry. The Queen has separate royal households in Scotland and Canada.

Among the more unusual positions are:

THE QUEEN'S PIPER

The sovereign has awakened each morning to the sound of bagpipes since Queen Victoria appointed the first piper in 1843. Queen Elizabeth the Queen Mother also had a piper, whose duty was to play at her request.

MARKER OF THE SWANS

All mute swans in open water in Britain are officially owned by the sovereign, and the holder of this post, established in the twelfth century, organizes the annual "swan upping," when unmarked birds are ringed.

OFFICIAL HARPIST TO THE PRINCE OF WALES

The harp is the national instrument of Wales. The post of official harpist lapsed during the reign of Queen Victoria but was revived in 2000 by Prince Charles, the current prince of Wales.

LOYAL TO THE ROYALS

Each year at Christmas, the sovereign presents every member of the royal household with a traditional Christmas pudding and a gift. The value of the gift is determined by length of service.

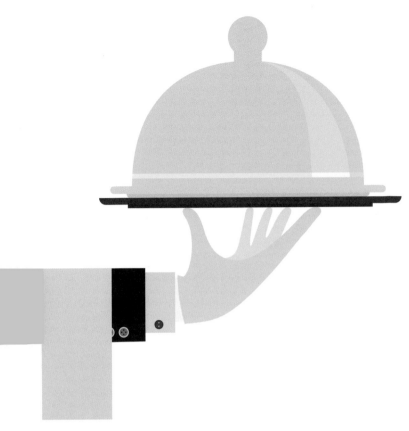

UPSTAIRS, DOWNSTAIRS

Upper- and middle-class Victorian households were run like small businesses, staffed according to size, location, and the family income. Even modest households would have at least a maid-of-all-work. Reflecting upstairs society as a whole, a strict hierarchy operated downstairs.

MAIN HOUSEHOLD STAFF

FIRST LEVEL

Butler
Head of the male staff; in charge of the wine cellar, supervising family dining and social events, employing and supervising footmen and other male staff. In larger households, he was supported by an under butler.

Housekeeper
Head of the female staff; in charge of running the household, cleaning, maintenance, household accounts, liaison with tradesmen, and supervising the maids' work.

SECOND LEVEL

Valet (aka Groom of the Chamber)

Attended to all personal needs of the master of the house, preparing his clothes, helping him to wash, shave, and dress.

Lady's Maid

Attended to all the needs of the mistress and her wardrobe, including hairdressing.

THIRD LEVEL

Footman

Responsible for the footwear, polishing the silver, answering the door, and assisting the butler. Large households would include a first footman, a lady's footman, and a number of under footmen. Footmen were usually required to be fit specimens of manhood who looked good in a uniform, to add style to a household.

Housemaids

Responsible for cleaning all the rooms, preparing and lighting fires, changing bed linen, and emptying the chamber pots. Chambermaids were responsible for the bedrooms and parlor maids for the living and reception rooms. In larger households there would be under housemaids or a second and third housemaid.

Laundry Maid

Responsible for washing and cleaning the family's clothes and bed linen. Laundry maids might live out and come in as and when required.

SUB DEPARTMENTS

THE KITCHEN

Although the housekeeper and butler had seniority in the kitchen, in practice it was the province of the cook. The quality of the cook could make or break a household's social standing.

Cook

Responsible for cooking meals for the family, guests, and servants, supervising kitchen staff, and planning menus (with the butler and housekeeper).

Kitchen Maid

Assistant to the cook, responsible for the cleanliness of the kitchen and food preparation; large households could maintain several kitchen maids.

Scullery Maid

The scullery was a small room at the back of the kitchen used for washing up. The scullery maid was a kitchen dogsbody, subordinate to the kitchen maids, responsible for washing up and cleaning pots.

Houseboy
A boy who waited on the other servants.

Households with children maintained nursery staff.

Head Nurse / Nanny
In charge of the family's babies and children until the girls were old enough for a governess

and the boys were sent away to school. A large family would require under nurses as well.

Nursery Maid
Responsible for cleaning the nursery, washing diapers, and so on.

OUTSIDE STAFF

Coachman
Responsible for the overall functioning of the stables and the driving and maintenance of the family coach. A large household could also have had an under coachman.

Groom
Responsible for grooming the horses.

Stable Boy
Subject to orders from the groom and coachman, responsible for mucking out the stables.

Head Gardener
Responsible for the grounds, garden, and greenhouses; planning and planting flowers and vegetables; providing cut flowers for the house and produce for the kitchen.

Under Gardener
Under orders from the head gardener.

Laborers
Employed on an ad hoc basis for heavy work in the garden.

NEITHER FISH NOR FOWL
Governesses, employed to educate the girls of the family, occupied an ambiguous social position; they were not considered actual servants, as they were often the poorer members of middle-class families.

ORDERS OF CHIVALRY

Twice a year—at New Year's and on the Queen's official birthday in June—*The Gazette* publishes a list of recipients of what is sometimes referred to colloquially as a "gong"—an honorary award for exceptional achievement or service in the UK or any of the Commonwealth countries, listed on the following spread in descending order of importance. With the exception of the most ancient orders, whose members are chosen by the sovereign, nominations for the awards are made either by government departments or by members of the public.

THE MOST NOBLE ORDER OF THE GARTER

The oldest order of chivalry, inspired by tales of King Arthur's Knights of the Round Table and originally for male aristocrats only. Members are styled Knight or Lady of the Garter.

Founded by / date: Edward III / 1348

Who: Men and women

Why: Recognition of public service

Number of members: Twenty-four knights + members of royal family

Motto: *Honi soit qui mal y pense* ("Shame on him who thinks this evil")

Designatory letters: KG/LG

THE MOST ANCIENT AND MOST NOBLE ORDER OF THE THISTLE

The origins of this Scottish order of knighthood are unclear, but it may have been founded in the fifteenth century by James III of Scotland, who adopted the thistle as the royal plant. The order was revived in 1687 by James VII of Scotland (James II of England), lapsed when he was deposed, and was revived again by Queen Anne in 1703. Members are styled Knight or Lady of the Thistle.

Founded by / date: James III / fifteenth century

Who: Scottish men and women

Why: Significant contribution to national life

Number of members: Sixteen + members of royal family

Motto: *Nemo me impune lacessit* ("No one provokes me with impunity")

Designatory letters: KT/LT

THE MOST HONORABLE ORDER OF THE BATH

The curious name derives from the purification ritual of bathing that once formed part of the knighthood ceremony. There are three grades (see below).

Founded by / date: George I / 1725

Who: Men and women

Why: Military service or exemplary civilian merit

Grades (number of members): Knight/Dame Grand Cross (120), Knight/Dame Commander (355), Companion (1,925)

Motto: *Tria juncta in uno* ("Three joined in one")

Designatory letters:
Knight/Dame Grand Cross—GCB
Knight/Dame Commander—KCB/DCB
Companion—CB

KNIGHTS BACHELOR

A "men only" knight-hood, not attached to any particular order of chivalry. This most ancient but also most lowly knightly honor is often awarded to those in the world of sport or entertainment. Knights Bachelor are styled "Sir" but have no designatory letters.

THE ORDER OF MERIT

Comparable to the French Legion d'Honneur and the American Congressional Gold Medal. Although there is no knighthood attached to the honor, its exclusivity and prestigious reputation make it highly desirable.

Founded by / date: Edward VII / 1902

Who: Men and women

Why: Exceptional distinction in the armed forces or the fields of arts, sciences, and learning

Number of members: Twenty-four

Motto: "For merit"

Designatory letters: OM

COMPANION OF HONOR

A sort of "junior" Order of Merit, this award was created to recognize services of national importance.

Founded by / date: George V / 1917

Who: Men and women

Why: Contribution to the arts, science, medicine, or government over a long period

Number of members: Sixty-five

Motto: "In action faithful and in honor clear"

Designatory letters: CH

THE MOST DISTINGUISHED ORDER OF ST. MICHAEL AND ST. GEORGE

Founded to recognize distinguished citizens of the Ionian Islands (now part of Greece, but at that time under British protection) and Malta. There are three grades (listed below).

Founded by / date: Prince Regent George IV / 1818

Who: Men and women

Why: Service in a foreign country or in relation to foreign or Commonwealth affairs

Grades (number of members): Knight/Dame Grand Cross (125), Knight/Dame Commander (375), Companion (1,750)

Motto: *Auspicium melioris aevi* ("Token of a better age")

Designatory letters:

Knight/Dame Grand Cross—GCMG

Knight/Dame Commander—KCMG/DCMG

Companions—CMG

ROYAL VICTORIAN ORDER

Instituted by Queen Victoria in 1896, it rewards personal services rendered to the monarch. There are five grades (listed below).

Founded by / date: Queen Victoria / 1896

Who: Men and women

Why: Personal services rendered to the monarch

Number of members: Unlimited

Grades: Knight/Dame Grand Cross, Knight/Dame Commander, Commander, Lieutenant, Member

Motto: Victoria

Designatory letters:

Knight/Dame Grand Cross— GCVO

Knight/Dames Commander— KCVO/DCVO

Commander—CVO

Lieutenant—LVO

Member—MVO

THE MOST EXCELLENT ORDER OF THE BRITISH EMPIRE

Founded to recognize ordinary people who rendered service to the nation, both military and civilian, originally during World War I. The majority of people receiving a "gong" will be admitted to one of the five grades (see opposite), of which the two highest are knighthoods.

Founded by / date: George V / 1917

Who: Men and women

Why: Exceptional achievement or service

Number of members: Unlimited

Grades: Knight/Dame Grand Cross, Knight/Dame Commander, Commander, Officer, Member

Motto: "For God and the Empire"

Designatory letters:

Knight/Dame Grand Cross—GBE

Knight/Dame Commander—KBE/ DBE

Commander—CBE

Officer—OBE

Member—MBE

FORM AN ORDERLY LINE

Since the Middle Ages, knighthood has been conferred in a ritual act known as "the accolade." In the UK, this takes the form of the sovereign (or delegate) dubbing the kneeling recipient on both shoulders with a sword. Queen Elizabeth II uses the sword that belonged to her father, George VI. Neither women receiving a damehood nor clergy receiving a knighthood are dubbed.

SIXTEENTH-CENTURY FASHION ETIQUETTE

On June 15, 1574, Elizabeth I reinforced the sumptuary laws (Enforcing Statutes of Apparel) laid down by her father, Henry VIII. Concerned that profligate spending on the latest ruff would lead to "the manifest decay of the whole realm" along with "the wasting and undoing of a great number of young gentlemen," the strict laws also ensured that everyone who was anyone knew their place. They specified the color, material, and type of clothing each individual could wear, acting as a kind of sixteenth-century soccer uniform, ensuring the onlooker could identify others as "one of us"—signaling their rank and privilege at a glance. Transgressions were rewarded with harsh punishment, via fines and loss of property or title, although to begin with the queen in her "princely clemency" was content simply to "give warning to her loving subjects to reform themselves."

PURPLE SILK, "CLOTH OF GOLD TISSUED," SABLE FUR

Only to be worn by the king and queen and certain of their immediate family (including the king's mother). Permissible for dukes, marquises, and earls, but only in certain garments (doublets, jerkins, cloak linings, gowns, hose); Knights of the Garter could wear purple in mantles only.

CLOTH OF GOLD, SILVER, TINSELED SATIN, SILK, CLOTH MIXED OR EMBROIDERED WITH ANY GOLD OR SILVER

For viscounts and above only, also barons and "other persons of like degree" provided it was in doublets, jerkins, cloak linings, gowns, and hose.

WOOLEN CLOTH "MADE OUT OF THE REALM" (I.E., IMPORTED) IN CAPS ONLY; CRIMSON OR SCARLET VELVET; CERTAIN BLACK FURS; EMBROIDERY OR TAILOR'S WORK INVOLVING GOLD OR SILVER OR PEARLS

Limited to dukes, marquises, earls and their children, viscounts, barons, and "knights being companions of the Garter, or any person being of the Privy Council."

HARDWARE

"GILT, SILVERED OR DAMASKED" SPURS, SWORDS, RAPIERS, DAGGERS, CERTAIN KNIVES, BUCKLES OR GIRDLES, GILT

Only to be sported by knights and barons' sons, and above, and also by "gentlemen in ordinary office attendant upon the Queen's majesty's person"…providing they left their spurs at home.

DRESSING UP AND DOWN

On any occasion where dress code is specified, it's male attire that drives the choice of outfit. The rules on color, style, and accessories are often rigid, while women are given vague guidelines but left to create their own sartorial triumphs—or disasters. Here's how the hierarchy works, from the smartest to the (relatively) scruffiest.

WHITE TIE

The strictest, very definitely the starchiest, but ultimately the least likely to be required, although until World War II white tie was evening dress de rigueur for gentlemen. With the exception of the black dress trousers, tailcoat, and shoes (and of course socks), everything is white: dress shirt (including studs and cufflinks), detachable wing collar, bow tie, waistcoat. Women attending a white-tie occasion are required to wear full-length, formal evening dress, traditionally with long white gloves. Married women may wear a tiara, and all women can go to town with jewelry.

BLACK TIE

Still formal, still a bit starchy, and still in regular use for evening events. Black is the predominant color—for the dinner jacket (aka a DJ, or tuxedo), trousers, shoes, socks, shirt studs, and of course the bow tie, which English etiquette guide Debrett's advises should be "proportionate to the size of the wearer." Only the evening shirt is white, with a turn-down collar, and please—no ruffles. Women have far more choice here (and therefore far more scope to get it wrong!)— a long evening dress or skirt, or a knee-length cocktail dress, or even wide-legged trousers worn with a flowing top.

MORNING DRESS

Formal day dress, as the name suggests—it is never worn at events starting after six o'clock in the evening. A black or gray morning coat is worn with gray or gray-and-black-striped trousers, a white or pale-colored shirt, and a waistcoat—all the buttons done up if double-breasted, or with the lowest button undone if single-breasted. A tie is worn rather than a cravat, and the top hat is only worn at the races; otherwise, it's carried. Women wear something smart and modest—a dress or skirt with a tailored jacket, daytime jewelry such as pearls, and, to complete the outfit—depending on the occasion—a hat.

LOUNGE SUITS

Despite the rather smart description, just a general-purpose suit and tie, which are worn for business and slightly formal social events. The style of suit is down to the wearer's prefer-ence—three-piece, which includes a waistcoat, or two-piece, without a waistcoat. And standards must still be observed—the shirt must be worn with a tie, and the top button must be

done up. Women wear a toned-down version of their morning dress outfit.

SMART CASUAL

Not as simple as it sounds, not only because there's far more choice but also because there's formal smart casual and informal smart casual. *Formal* means smart separates with a casual shirt rather than a suit, and definitely no jeans; *informal* means the same, but smart jeans are permitted, and a polo shirt. T-shirts and sneakers do not constitute smart casual. The same applies to women, who should avoid anything resembling business wear but also shun sports-wear and sneakers. Debrett's advice is: If in doubt, ask your host or hostess for guidance.

TRADITIONAL WEDDING ANNIVERSARY GIFTS BY YEAR

In a tradition that dates back to the Middle Ages, anniversary gifts are given in increasing value to symbolize the preciousness of the couple's growing bond.

Year 1:	Paper
Year 2:	Cotton
Year 3:	Leather
Year 4:	Linen and Silk (or Fruit and Flowers)
Year 5:	Wood
Year 6:	Iron/Candy
Year 7:	Wool/Copper
Year 8:	Pottery/Bronze
Year 9:	Pottery (or Willow)
Year 10:	Tin/Aluminum
Year 11:	Steel
Year 12:	Silk (or Linen)
Year 13:	Lace
Year 14:	Ivory (or Gold Jewelry)
Year 15:	Crystal
Year 20:	China
Year 25:	Silver
Year 30:	Pearl
Year 35:	Coral
Year 40:	Ruby
Year 45:	Sapphire
Year 50:	Gold
Year 55:	Emerald

Year 60: Diamond—This was originally for the seventy-fifth anniversary, but when Queen Victoria celebrated her Diamond Jubilee during her sixtieth year on the royal throne, they changed it to the sixtieth year.

DIVIDE AND RULE

There is an agreed "order of operations" in mathematics, starting with the calculations inside brackets, and then descending via those involving indices (roots and square roots) and division and multiplication to the easier operations of addition and subtraction. The acronym BIDMAS helps you work out the order in which the law applies to different elements of a complicated operation. Let's take it from the top:

First do all the calculations in **B**rackets.
Then tackle the **I**ndices (powers such as squares, square roots).

Next do the **D**ivision and **M**ultiplication (start on the left and work them out in the order you find them).

And lastly, do the **A**ddition and **S**ubtraction (when only addition and subtraction are left, work them out in the order you find them, again starting from the left).

THEREFORE
$4 + 2 \times 4 = 24$ (wrong: do not add $4 + 2$ and then multiply $\times 4$)
$4 + 2 \times 4 = 12$ (correct: multiply 2×4 and then add 4)
$6 \times (5 + 3) = 33$ (wrong: do not multiply 6×5 and then add 3)
$6 \times (5 + 3) = 48$ (correct: do brackets first so 8×6)

Division and multiplication are regarded as being on the same level; this also applies to addition and subtraction—in both cases, complete the calculations in the order of left to right:
$7 - 2 + 6 = 11$
$4 \div 2 \times 5 = 10$

MNEMONICS
BIDMAS is sometimes known as BODMAS (O = order, numbers involving square roots or powers). In the USA it is known as PEMDAS (Parentheses, Exponents, Multiplication, Division, Addition, and Subtraction, or to commit to memory more whimsically, "Please Excuse My Dear Aunt Sally" or "Please Enter Math Data As Shown").

POKER HAND HIERARCHY

Poker is a game of cards played with a standard fifty-two-card deck, and betting is a key element in winning. There are many variants of the game, but the same basic rules apply to all: Five or seven cards are dealt in a variety of ways to each of the players, who then try to form the best poker hand possible. The eventual winner may not necessarily have the best hand; it is enough to convince your opponents that you are unbeatable, at which point they will fold, cutting their losses and ceding you victory by default. Players should seek not to give away clues about the true nature of the cards they hold, hence the term *poker face*. The same hierarchy of hands is used by most variants of the game, which has enjoyed something of a comeback recently, and online poker is now hugely popular with both players and spectators.

1. ROYAL FLUSH
A, K, Q, J, 10, all the same suit.

2. STRAIGHT FLUSH
Five cards in a sequence, all in the same suit.

3. FOUR OF A KIND
All four cards of the same rank.

4. FULL HOUSE
Three of a kind with a pair.

5. FLUSH
Any five cards of the same suit, but not in a sequence.

6. STRAIGHT
Five cards in a sequence, but not of the same suit.

7. THREE OF A KIND
Three cards of the same rank.

8. TWO PAIR
Two different pairs.

9. PAIR
Two cards of the same rank.

10. HIGH CARD
When you haven't made any of the hands above, the highest card plays.

LEVELS OF G NETWORKS

Generations of wireless cellular technology are known as G networks. Each iteration of these networks has increased our ability to connect our phones to the world.

_____

1G

Launched in the early 1980s, 1G was a voice-only analog network that was similar to a radio trans-mission, which meant it could be intercepted. At its peak, there were close to 2 million users.

2G

Introduced in the early 1990s, the digital 2G network allowed cell phones to text, and send pictures and longer messages, as well as make calls more protected from interception. The downside was that digital service was limited by the cell tower range.

3G

Introduced in 1998, 3G allowed users the ability to access the internet, which meant they could send emails, search the web, FaceTime, download videos, and use apps that require data, all at a much faster speed. The issues continued to be coverage, speed, and dropped calls.

4G

Released in 2008, 4G has all of the capabilities of 3G but is ten times faster, with 100 megabits per second. Mainly available in large cities, these speeds could surpass broadband, as well as support high-tech features such as HD mobile TV and gaming.

LTE (4G LTE)

Standing for "long term evolu-tion," LTE is a form of 4G that enables even faster speeds.

5G

In 2020 or sooner, data will be available at faster speeds, with lower latency (or delay of data), and increased bandwidth. Processed at 1–10 gigabits per seconds, the speed of this network can help refine self-driving cars, virtual reality, and even health care apps.

CAR CLASS

MINICOMPACT
Interior Size: Less than 85 cubic feet

Examples: Mini Cooper, Volkswagen Beetle

SUBCOMPACT
Interior Size: 85–99 cubic feet

Examples: Toyota Prius, Honda CR-Z, Chevrolet Spark

COMPACT
Interior Size: 100–109 cubic feet

Examples: Honda Civic, Kia Soul, Mazda Mazda3

MIDSIZE
Interior Size: 110–119 cubic feet

Examples: Chevrolet Malibu, Nissan Altima, Toyota Camry

SUV CLASS

COMPACT CROSSOVER
Interior Size: Less than 124 cubic feet

Examples: Jeep Compass, Nissan X-Trail

CROSSOVER
Interior Size: 25–140 cubic feet

Examples: Subaru Crosstrek, Lincoln MKC

SIZE OF CARS

With so many different shapes and models of cars tooling down the highway, it's hard to keep track of types.

LARGE
Interior Size: More than 120 interior cubic feet

Examples: Nissan Maxima, Chevrolet Impala, Ford Taurus

SMALL WAGON
Interior Size: 130 interior cubic feet

Examples: Chevrolet Sonic, Honda Fit

LARGE WAGON
Interior Size: 160 interior cubic feet

Examples: Nissan Murano, Volvo V90

MIDSIZE
Interior Size: 41–170 cubic feet

Examples: Toyota Highlander, Jeep Grand Cherokee, Ford Explorer

FULL-SIZE
Interior Size: Less than 170 cubic feet

Examples: Chevrolet Suburban or Tahoe, Cadillac Escalade, Dodge Durango

TRUCK CLASS

MIDSIZE
Midsize trucks come in regular, extended, and crew sizes, and have less horsepower than full-size trucks.

Examples: Chevrolet Colorado, GMC Canyon

FULL-SIZE
These trucks also come in regular, extended, and crew sizes, and have more power than smaller trucks and SUVs.

Examples: Chevrolet Silverado, Ford F-150

CREDITWORTHINESS

Credit scores are awarded not just to individuals—most people only find out they have one when they are unexpectedly turned down for a loan—but also to companies and countries. Several credit ratings agencies (Standard & Poor's, Fitch Ratings, and Moody's) cover some 95 percent of the ratings market between them. They award a letter score to debt issued by a corporation or government on the basis of that particular institution's creditworthiness (how likely they are to repay a debt) and vulnerability (how likely they are to default); higher grades indicate lower chances of default.

There is a range of systems for short-term debt, but for long-term lending, a typical rating would range from AAA to D (with lowercase letters and +/– signs sometimes added for fine-tuning, as detailed below).

PRIME
AAA (an extremely good capacity for repayment)

HIGH GRADE
AA+, AA, AA– (a very strong capacity)

UPPER-MEDIUM GRADE
A+, A, A– (a strong capacity)

LOWER-MEDIUM GRADE
BBB+, BBB, BBB– (an adequate capacity)

NON-INVESTMENT GRADE (SPECULATIVE)
BB+, BB, BB– (vulnerable and open to default)

HIGHLY SPECULATIVE
B+, B, B– (vulnerable and more likely to default)

INVOLVING SUBSTANTIAL RISK
CCC+, CCC, CCC– (currently vulnerable)

EXTREMELY SPECULATIVE
CC (currently highly vulnerable)

AT RISK OF IMMINENT DEFAULT
C (currently highly vulnerable, default likely)

IN DEFAULT
DDD, DD, D (the debtor has failed to pay an obligation)

FROM A TO D

These ratings are extremely important in determining how much interest countries have to offer on the debt they issue—essentially, it is an indicator of how much they have to pay to access credit markets. But no country is immune to the ignominy of having their rating downgraded. Political and economic upheaval mean that even normally stable countries can be stripped of their triple-A ratings by one or more of the agencies, as has happened to the UK, USA, Finland, and France.

THE EBAY STAR SYSTEM

Feedback stars on the online auction and trading company eBay, launched by Pierre Omidyar in 1995, appear next to a member's user ID and are awarded based on feedback. The higher the score, the more positive ratings a member has been awarded.

STAR COLOR	RATING
Yellow	10 to 49
Blue	50 to 99
Turquoise	100 to 499
Purple	500 to 999
Red	1,000 to 4,999
Green	5,000 to 9,999
Yellow shooting star	10,000 to 24,999
Turquoise shooting star	25,000 to 49,999
Purple shooting star	50,000 to 99,999
Red shooting star	100,000 to 499,999
Green shooting star	500,000 to 999,999
Silver shooting star	1,000,000 or more

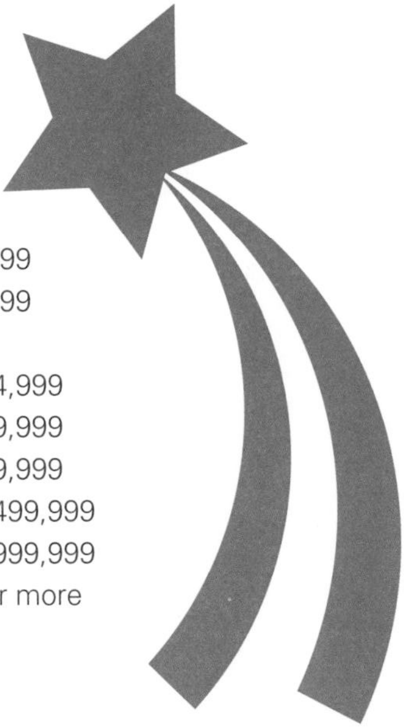

MARKETING EFFECTS

In 1961 Robert J. Lavidge and Gary A. Steiner devised this hierarchy designed to assist the era's *Mad Men* in guiding consumers through the various stages of purchasing to clinch that all-important deal, whether it be a bar of chocolate or a premium-brand luxury car. This "management speak" hierarchy is still in use today.

COGNITIVE STAGE
The consumer becomes aware of and gathers knowledge about a product.

Awareness
Make consumers aware of your brand/product. A no-brainer; consumers must be aware that your product exists in order to buy it.

Knowledge
Ensure information about your product and how it can be of value to the consumer is out there and readily available.

AFFECTIVE STAGE
Emotions start to play a part and the consumer begins (hopefully) to find themselves drawn to your product/brand.

Liking
Build a liking for the product with consumers. Make sure any possible reservations are firmly dealt with by the marketing.

Preference
The consumer likes your product (good) but is now considering it alongside others (introducing an element of risk), evaluating their advantages and disadvantages. Now is the time to emphasize your product's unique selling points.

CONATIVE STAGE
After weighing the pros and cons, the consumer takes action and reaches for their wallet.

Conviction
The consumer is about to make a decision; any doubt about opting for your product in the (possibly wavering) consumer's mind must be quashed. Hand out free samples, discount vouchers, and so on…something to help the consumer decide and remain faithful to your product postpurchase rather than switch flightily to the next brand that offers a special deal.

Purchase
Make this easy (multiple paying options) and enjoyable (ensure the product is available and attractively displayed, special offers to make the consumer feel good, etc.). Make it a pleasurable experience for the consumer and they may come back for more. Hooked. Job done!

MASLOW'S HIERARCHY OF NEEDS

A well-known system developed by American humanistic psychologist Abraham Maslow and first published in 1943, it ranks our fundamental motivations, from the basics needed to survive. The first four are described as deficiency needs and the fifth (self-actualization) as a growth need. Once one level is satisfied, the desire to move on to the next kicks in. Managers use the hierarchy as a motivational tool, to identify and fulfill the needs of their staff.

ORIGINAL

1 Physiological
Air, food and drink, sleep, sex, warmth.

2 Safety
Security and freedom from fear.

3 Social needs
A sense of belonging and love, friendship, and company.

4 Esteem
Social recognition and prestige, respect from others, personal worth.

5 Self-actualization
Achieving one's full potential, including creatively.

EXTENDED

In the alternative-culture-led 1960s and 1970s, three more stages were slotted into the order:

4 (a) Cognitive—knowledge and understanding, curiosity, exploration, meaning.

4 (b) Aesthetic—appreciation and search for beauty, balance, etc.

6 Transcendence—helping others to achieve self-actualization.

MILLENNIUM UPDATE
Some people might add "internet connection" to the list...

HAZARD CONTROL

A "health and safety" system devised to deal with potential hazards in industry and the workplace, minimizing or ideally removing exposure to hazards altogether.

ELIMINATE
Remove the cause of the risk completely by changing a work process. For example, use equipment to move heavy items rather than have workers move them manually.

SUBSTITUTE
Replace a hazardous practice/ item with a safe alternative. For example, replace a substance used in powder form (hazardous particles may be inhaled) with one in crystal or pellet form.

ENGINEER CONTROLS
Methods built into the design of a plant or working process to isolate people at risk from the hazard. For example, reduce noise levels with noise-dampening equipment.

ADMINISTRATIVE CONTROLS
Limit workers' exposure to a hazard or change their behavior. For example, rotating schedules to limit their exposure to a hazard; installing warning signs so they'll avoiding touching their eyes, lips, or nose with contaminated hands.

PERSONAL PROTECTIVE EQUIPMENT (PPE)
Such as gloves, ear defenders, hard hats, and high-visibility jackets to control the hazard. The least effective method and the last resort, since protective equipment may fail (leak/break) without warning.

1984

George Orwell's prescient and gloomy view of the future was published in 1949 but remains relevant today. His dystopian society where citizens are watched, tortured if they dare to think differently, and brainwashed into "right thinking" is a chilling portrait of a state accountable to none or run by a despotic ruler.

BIG BROTHER
Head of the totalitarian super state Oceania.

INNER PARTY (2 PERCENT OF THE POPULATION)
"The Party" is the ruling class that governs and makes policy decisions. Members join the Party by passing an exam— "The Party is not concerned with perpetuating its blood but with perpetuating itself."

They enjoy certain privileges such as being able to turn off the "telescreens" that watch them, have servants, access to coffee and tea, and comfortable homes.

OUTER PARTY
An educated class, they administrate and implement the Party's policies but have no say in making them. They live in inferior homes, eat inferior food, and are under constant supervision. They are also encouraged to inform on any non-right-thinking party members.

They have access to Victory cigarettes and gin (rather than wine). They must abstain from sex other than to procreate.

PROLES (85 PERCENT OF THE POPULATION)
The workers perform menial tasks and labor, and are kept uneducated, but they are not watched, as they are not deemed sufficiently worthy.

They are fed entertainment ("prolefeed") such as films, trashy novels, sports, and pornography to keep the unthinking masses happy.

ANIMAL FARM

Orwell's satire on society in Russia following the 1917 revolution was published in 1945. It describes how the animals (the working class) rebel against the cruel and neglectful farmer (the Tsar) and his men, and drive them out. Once alone, the pigs draw up the Seven Commandments of Animalism, including the premise that "All animals are equal," and start out to make a just society. But eventually the pigs begin to emerge as the most intelligent and start to take over, with pig-in-chief Napoleon as leader.

NAPOLEON (STALIN)
A large male Berkshire pig and the supreme leader, before whom everyone has to bow.

ALL OTHER PIGS (STALIN'S MINISTERS)
Who do Napoleon's bidding.

THE DOGS (RUSSIAN SECRET POLICE)
They maintain law and order, ostensibly for the whole farm, but in reality spend most of their time protecting and working for Napoleon.

ALL THE OTHER ANIMALS (THE WORKING CLASS)
Despite their strength in numbers they must obey the leader and the system without question.

THE HANDMAID'S TALE

A dystopian novel by Margaret Atwood set in a near future in Cambridge, Massachusetts, now part of the Republic of Gilead, a totalitarian theocratic state. In response to an unspecified environmental crisis, the birth rate has dropped below zero; the state's goal is to seize control of reproduction, and therefore of women and their bodies. Society is divided along rigid caste lines, with all women subservient to men but also split into castes themselves. This has the toxic effect of demolishing solidarity among them, denying empathy and encouraging the willingness of women to oppress other women. *The Handmaid's Tale* won the Arthur C. Clarke Award for the best science fiction novel in 1987.

Name	Role	Uniform	Benefits	Punishment
Commanders of the Faithful	Ruling class; entitled to Wife, Handmaid, Marthas, and Guardians.	Black.	Allowed to drive cars, read, dictate the law.	
Eyes of God	Secret police.	Usually in disguise.	To spy on everyone, including the elite.	
Angels	Soldiers.	Military uniform.	Allowed to marry.	
Guardians of the Faith	Routine police and guard work. Un-suitable for other work as stupid, old, or very young.	Green uniforms.	Young Guardians could be promoted to Angels when old enough.	
Gender Traitors	Homo-sexuals or other untraditional orienta-tions.			Hanged or sent to the Colonies.*

*The Colonies are areas outside the Republic of Gilead that are environmentally toxic. People sent there face certain, usually lingering, death.

Name	Role	Uniform	
Aunts	Unmarried, infertile, or older women trained to monitor and control other women, especially Handmaids and Jezebels.	Brown, with leather belts and armed with cattle prods.	
Handmaids	Young fertile women forced to bear children for Commanders and their Wives.	Red habits, gloves, and shoes, white bonnets with wings to hide their faces.	
Marthas	Older or infertile women without the Aunt mentality. Domestic duties: cooking, cleaning, child minding.	Green overalls.	
Wives	Wives of high-status men.	Blue dress.	
Econo-wives	Wives of low-status men. Have to perform all female rites: childbearing, domestic work, and companionship.	Red, blue, and green dress.	
Unwomen	Women who refuse or are unsuited for other roles: the sterile, some widows, nuns, lesbians, feminists, dissidents.		
Jezebels	Prostitutes and entertainers. Available only to Commanders and guests.	Dress as stereotypes: cheerleaders, sexy outfits.	

Benefits	Punishment
Confers the highest status.	
Better fed than others, but not allowed to wear makeup or socialize with men.	Sent to Colonies* if they do not produce a child after three two-year tours of duty.
High status.	No autonomy or function.
Allowed to wear makeup, drink, and socialize with men.	Sterilized. Work in regulated brothels. Rigidly controlled by the Aunts. Sent to the Colonies* when no longer attractive.

* The Colonies are areas outside the Republic of Gilead that are environmentally toxic. People sent there face certain, usually lingering, death.

SUPER MARIO BROS.

The character of Mario the plumber, originally a carpenter known as "Jumpman," first appeared in the Nintendo arcade game *Donkey Kong* in 1981, then with his brother Luigi in *Mario Bros.* in 1983. *Super Mario Bros.* was bundled with the release of the Nintendo Entertainment System in 1985 in the United States. It has since become one of the best-selling video games of all time, and Mario has gone on to appear in more than two hundred different video games.

Set in Mushroom World, the main premise of *Super Mario Bros.* is to save Princess Peach (also known as Princess Toadstool) from Bowser, an evil turtle who uses dark energy. To win *Super Mario Bros.* Mario or Luigi must defeat different enemies and obstacles in eight different worlds to rescue her.

Level	Setting	Opponents
1-1	Overworld	Goomba, Koopa Troopa
1-2	Underground	Goomba, Koopa Troopa, Piranha Plant
1-3	Athletic	Goomba, Koopa Troopa, Koopa Paratroopa
1-4	Castle	Fire Bar, Bowser Imposter (Goomba)
2-1	Overworld	Goomba, Koopa Troopa, Koopa Paratroopa, Piranha Plant
2-2	Underwater	Blooper, Cheep Cheep, Piranha Plant
2-3	Athletic	Cheep Cheep
2-4	Castle	Fire Bar, Lava Bubble, Bowser Imposter (Koopa Trooper)
3-1	Overworld	Goomba, Koopa Troopa, Koopa Paratroopa, Piranha Plant, Hammer Brother
3-2	Overworld	Goomba, Koopa Troopa, Koopa Paratroopa, Piranha Plant

3-3	Athletic	Goomba, Koopa Troopa, Koopa Paratroopa
3-4	Castle	Fire Bar, Lava Bubble, Bowser Impostor (Buzzy Beetle)
4-1	Overworld	Piranha Plant, Lakitu, Spiny
4-2	Underground	Goomba, Koopa Troopa, Piranha Plant, Buzzy Beetle
4-3	Athletic	Koopa Troopa, Koopa Paratroopa
4-4	Castle	Piranha Plant, Lava Bubble, Fire Bar, Bowser Imposter (Spiny)
5-1	Overworld	Goomba, Koopa Troopa, Koopa Paratroopa, Piranha Plant, Bullet Bill
5-2	Overworld	Goomba, Koopa Troopa, Koopa Paratroopa, Piranha Plant, Buzzy Beetle, Bullet Bill, Hammer Brother (Blooper, Cheep Cheep)
5-3	Athletic	Goomba, Koopa Troopa, Koopa Paratroopa, Bullet Bill
5-4	Castle	Lava Bubble, Fire Bar, Bowser Impostor (Lakitu)
6-1	Overworld	Piranha Plant, Lakitu, Spiny
6-2	Overworld	Goomba, Koopa Troopa, Koopa Paratroopa, Piranha Plant, Buzzy Beetle (Blooper, Cheep Cheep)
6-3	Athletic	Bullet Bill
6-4	Castle	Lava Bubble, Fire Bar, Bowser Impostor (Blooper)
7-1	Overworld	Koopa Troopa, Koopa Paratroopa, Piranha Plant, Buzzy Beetle, Hammer Brother, Bullet Bill
7-2	Underwater	Blopoper, Cheep Cheep, Piranha Plant
7-3	Athletic	Cheep Cheep, Koopa Troopa, Koopa Paratroopa
7-4	Castle	Lava Bubble, Fire Bar, Bowser Impostor (Hammer Brother)
8-1	Overworld	Goomba, Koopa Troopa, Koopa Paratroopa, Piranha Plant, Buzzy Beetle
8-2	Overworld	Goomba, Koopa Paratroopa, Piranha Plant, Buzzy Beetle, Lakitu, Spiny, Bullet Bill
8-3	Overworld	Koopa Troopa, Koopa Paratroopa, Piranha Plant, Bullet Bill, Hammer Brother
8-4	Castle (with an underwater section)	Goomba, Koopa Paratroopa, Piranha Plant, Fire Bar, Lava Bubble, Buzzy Beetle, Hammer Brother, Blooper, Cheep Cheep, Bowser

THE COWBOY CATTLE DRIVE

Cattle drives in the American West became large affairs following the American Civil War and with the expansion of the cattle industry. Between the 1860s and late 1880s, American cowboys operated an effective hierarchy of roles to aid communication and discipline during a drive, on which there could be around two to three thousand head of cattle to move long distances between states. The division of labor was generally as follows:

TRAIL BOSS

Responsible for the safety of the herd, keeping cattle and humans fed and watered, handling the money, and maintaining the peace. He would be paid around ninety dollars a month.

CHUCK WAGON COOK

Cooking three meals a day from the back of a chuck wagon, involving setting up and dismantling the "kitchen" three times a day with each new camp, was no easy feat. The cook was also responsible for the personal belongings of the cowboys. He drew the second-highest pay on a drive, around sixty bucks a month, and was not a guy to cross.

POINT MAN

Guided the direction of the herd on the trail. He also watched out for hazards such as rattlesnakes, coyotes, and thieves. The point man pocketed around thirty to forty dollars a month.

SWING

Kept the herd together and ensured the flanks were not threatened by coyotes or raiding parties. The swing would ride a third of the way back from the point man and was paid the same wage.

FLANK

Rode at the back to make sure slower cattle kept up with the herd. He was paid the same as the point man.

DRAG

Ensured that any slower cattle caught up with the herd and pushed the slower animals forward. A dusty, dirty, and unpleasant job usually reserved for new cowboys. The wage was around the same as the point man's.

WRANGLER

The horse wrangler looked after all the horses, kept them fed and well, and drove the remuda (herd of remount horses) ahead of the cattle. He would help the cook gather firewood and gathered around twenty-five dollars a month for himself.

FROM VAQUERO TO BUCKAROO

The original cowboys were the Mexican *vaqueros* (from the Spanish word *vaca*, meaning "cow"). They worked on ranches in Texas and Mexico. The English word *buckaroo* is an Anglicization of *vaquero*.

OIL RIGGED UP

Crews on oil drilling rigs operate in twelve-hour shifts with specific tasks and responsibilities. A typical organizational structure for a drill or rig crew is as follows:

RIG MANAGER
Supervisor of the entire operation, with responsibility for all personnel, financial, technical, and performance aspects of a rig.

DRILLER/RIG OPERATOR
Second-in-command to the rig manager, responsible for maintaining safety, supervising the crews, and troubleshooting problems.

DERRICKHAND
Works up to 25 meters (82 feet) above the rig floor on a platform or "monkey board" attached to the rig's derrick (the mast that supports the drilling equipment), guiding tubing and instruments in and out of the well; he also operates the drilling-fluid or "mud" system (the viscous drilling fluid used to carry rock chips to the surface).

MOTORHAND
Responsible for the maintenance and repair of engines and other machinery.

ROUGHNECK/ROUSTABOUT
An entry-level position on a rig with responsibility for cleaning pipelines, and assembling, maintaining, and repairing the drilling equipment.

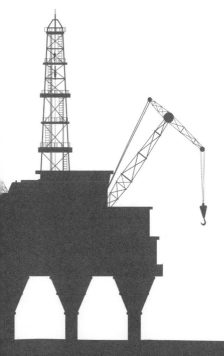

CLIMBING THE RIG LADDER
A "company man" or consultant is the on-site representative of the exploration company. "Tool pushers" work closely with the company man to ensure the rig has all the tools, equipment, and supplies it needs. Company men usually start as roustabouts and work their way up.

HIGHWAYS AND BYWAYS

Most countries' road systems evolved slowly over the centuries, at least until the arrival of the internal combustion engine. It was the proliferation of the motor car along with growing populations that forced countries to adapt and expand their road networks, often in an urgent and reactive rather than a planned and proactive way. Throw variations between regions and states into the mix, and it is not surprising that the numbering and classifying of roads has become a bone of contention for those who like a little order in their lives.

The Lancaster Turnpike, completed in 1795, was the first road to be engineered and planned in the USA. It connected Lancaster, Pennsylvania, with Philadelphia. One hundred and fifty years later, in 1956, construction of the interstate highway system was finally authorized, named the Dwight D. Eisenhower National System of Interstate and Defense Highways after its presidential champion.

INTERSTATE HIGHWAYS
State-to-state roads (limited access) that are numbered (e.g., I–48), and often divided by a median (central reservation). The major north–south routes have odd numbers and east–west routes even numbers. Interstates with three-digit numbers are bypasses, beltways (ring roads), or spurs off the main interstates.

U.S. STATE HIGHWAYS
Important national trunk roads connecting regions not served by the interstate highways. Numbered (e.g., US 32), they vary from two-lane roads to divided highways. Sometimes known as federal highways, they also follow the north–south/east–west odd/even numbers system.

STATE HIGHWAYS

These range from local back roads to major four-lane trunk roads, but most are two-lane highways. Also known as state routes. Each state/territory has its own system for numbering.

COUNTY ROADS

Secondary roads numbered according to the state's system. Known in some states (e.g., Texas) as farm or ranch roads. County roads vary greatly, from freeways and expressways to unpaved roads in remote areas.

OTHER ROADS

FREEWAY

Usually a toll-free divided highway with limited access via ramps; they enable traffic to flow unhindered (no traffic lights, crossroads/intersections, etc.). Interstate highways are also freeways.

EXPRESSWAY

A divided highway with limited access. Interstate, U.S., and state highways can also be expressways.

LIMITED-ACCESS ROAD

For high-speed traffic. Access is by ramp. There are no intersecting roads (other than those accessed by a ramp) and you can normally enter and exit only from the right.

PARKWAY

May be a scenic road or a good-standard toll road.

TURNPIKE

Usually a toll road of good standard (but may also be free).

FRONTAGE ROAD

Minor roads for local traffic, such as accessing motels and malls, farmland.

BUSINESS ROUTE

Divert off major roads to a town's business district.

SCENIC BYWAY

Any classification of road that offers fine views.

ULTIMATE ROAD TRIP

Although it runs from Santa Monica to Chicago, US 66, one of the most famous roads in the world, is not an interstate highway. Known as the Main Street of America in the 1930s because it ran through so many small towns, some segments were superseded by newer roads when the interstate highways were built, and it was ultimately decommissioned in 1985. Despite this, many organizations and individuals have preserved portions of it, and Route 66 can now be traveled again, but as a Historic Route.

THE TOUR DE FRANCE

Tactics loom large in the Tour de France, the most prestigious of the major cycle road races. Each team of nine riders works to promote their leader's chances of winning. The other eight riders take it in turns to take the energy-sapping hit of being exposed to wind resistance at the front. Those behind ride in the slipstream, conserving energy. Small groups of three to six near the front may attack by accelerating quickly to break away in an attempt to open up a gap ahead of the peloton, the main pack of riders. The hierarchy is fluid and may even change during a race, depending on whether the team is going for an overall win or just a stage win and how well the riders are going. And some of the rankings double up; for example, a rouleur may also be a super-domestique.

A TYPICAL TOUR TEAM

Team leader
The rider deemed to have the best chance of winning overall. Usually a good climber and time trialist.

Super-domestique (aka lieutenant)
A rider who remains with the team leader for as long as possible during challenging stages.

Sprinter
A rider who is good at sprinting (fast acceleration over short periods). May be allowed to go alone for a stage win on flat stages. Some teams are based around a sprinter, so they are also the team leader.

Rouleur (a good all-rounder)
A strong, powerful rider, good on flat sections (may also be a super-domestique).

Lead-out rider
A rider who is good at sprinting, but who may not have the explosive power of the best sprinter in the team. They aim to get the best sprinter into a position near the finish line.

To win a stage: about 3 kilometers before the finish, a lead-out train is formed by a line of four or five riders with the best sprinter at the back. The leading rider in the train cycles as fast as possible, then peels off when tired to let

the next rider do the same, and so on until the best sprinter is left to go for the finish line.

Grimpeur ("climber")
A rider who is good at ascents (mountains!). The grimpeur may be allowed to go alone for a stage win on mountain stages, but may also be asked to be a lead-out rider for the team leader on similar stages.

Domestique ("servant")
He supports the team through tactics (forming or chasing down breakaways and attacks). The domestique creates a slipstream for the team leader and obtains water/food from the support vehicle for the rest of his teammates en route, like a superfast waiter!

The jerseys are awarded to the leading riders in each category up to that point in the race, so the riders wearing them can change daily.

Maillot jaune (yellow jersey)
The prized yellow jersey is worn by the leader, the rider who has the lowest time overall in the race so far.

Maillot vert (green jersey)
Earned by the rider who has the most sprint points—points are awarded per day to the first riders across the line on the stage sprints and for time trials at certain sections along the route.

Maillot à pois (polka-dot jersey, white with red dots)
The "king of the mountains" wears this distinctive jersey for having earned the most points in the climbing stages.

Maillot blanc (white jersey)
Worn by the rider under twenty-five years of age with the lowest time overall at that point.

White-on-red identification number (instead of black-on-white)
The rider with the most "fighting spirit" points—earned for attacking moves.

Yellow number (instead of white)
Awarded to the leading team, based on the lowest total time of the first three riders in each team.

Rainbow jersey (band of colored horizontal stripes across a white background)
Worn by the world champion in a particular race discipline (time trial, sprint, etc.)—not specific to the Tour de France.

Unofficial award
The "Lanterne Rouge" ("red light") is the last rider to complete the race. Just completing the Tour de France is a huge achievement, so although the long list of runners-up is soon forgotten, the very last rider is often remembered.

FORMULA RACING

The art of racing open-wheeled single-seater cars is governed by the FIA (Federation Internationale de l'Automobile) and named after the FIA's "formulae," rules that the cars and race teams must comply with. The FIA tinkers with the detail each season, to keep everyone, spectators included, on their toes. The FIA's global pathway is designed to allow the best drivers to progress from karting through F4, F3, and F2 to compete in the F1 World Championship, without being distracted by other championship series along the way.

FORMULA 1

Inaugurated in 1950, the jewel in the Formula crown, the fastest road-course racing cars compete in the most glamorous and well known of all motorsport races. The cars are made by a handful of different manufacturers and must comply with the strict technical specifications. New circuits have been added over recent years, but changes were expected after new owners Liberty Media took over in 2017.

FORMULA 2

Replaced in 1985 by Formula 3000, F2 had a brief revival in 2009, was discontinued again in 2012, but made a comeback in 2017 when the FIA and the former GP2 series organization agreed to create "the ultimate training ground" for F1 in a new FIA F2 championship.

EUROPEAN FORMULA 3

Inaugurated in 1966, all Formula 3 cars must be stock block (built from a production model) with two-liter engines built by different manufacturers.

FORMULA 4

For drivers aged fifteen and over and launched in 2014, F4 aims to keep things low-cost to help young drivers take their first step up from karting. Drivers race in national and regional championships.

GP SERIES

Conceived by former F1 CEO Bernie Ecclestone and Flavio Briatore, the GP2 series was introduced in 2005 after the discontinuation of the FIA's feeder series Formula 3000, and the GP3 series was launched in 2010. Many champion drivers serve their apprenticeship with GP2.

PRIORITY AT SEA

The International Regulations for Preventing Collisions at Sea (aka COLREGS), based on a British system dating from 1862, have been adopted by most maritime states. This order of priority, designed to prevent a seagoing Mexican standoff, is determined by the vessels' function at the time of the meeting and by their position with relation to each other, and applies only when each has physical sight of the other (radar or sound signals are therefore excluded). The function of a boat is always contingent, so a fishing vessel is only a fishing vessel when its nets are out; on its way back to port, for example, it is classed merely as a power-driven vessel.

No vessel has absolute "right of way" and the rules apply anywhere at sea but may be subject to local by-laws. A "stand on" vessel maintains course and speed, proceeding unhindered, and a "give way" vessel maneuvers to keep clear. Deciding which vessel is which depends upon a wide range of factors, including each boat's method of propulsion, its position relative to the wind, its capability to maneuver, and even its particular function at the time.

NOT UNDER COMMAND (NUC)
A vessel that is unable to maneuver and keep out of the way of other vessels due to exceptional circumstances, such as engine failure.

RESTRICTED IN ABILITY TO MANEUVER (RAM)
A vessel that, due to the nature of her work (e.g., dredging, laying cables), is less able to maneuver and keep out of the way of other vessels.

CONSTRAINED BY DRAFT (CBD)

A power-driven vessel that is restricted in her ability to maneuver due to her draft (distance between the waterline and the bottom of a boat's hull) in relation to the available depth and width of navigable water.

FISHING VESSELS

Vessels engaged in fishing.

VESSELS POWERED BY SAIL

From dinghies to oceangoing super yachts.

POWER-DRIVEN VESSELS

Includes sailboats under power.

EXCEPTIONS

UNDER SAIL

Port tack boats must give way to starboard tack.

Boats on the same tack—the boat to windward must take evasive action.

MOTOR-DRIVEN

Boats meeting head on—both turn to starboard. Make a sound signal—one short blast.

Two power-driven vessels crossing—the boat which has the other on her starboard side shall keep out of the way.

KNOTTY SUBJECT

In open water overtaking may be carried out either to port or to starboard, providing proper notice has been given (sound signals) and the boat to be overtaken has consented and taken appropriate measures. In a narrow channel, overtaking is usually carried out on the port side, if absolutely necessary; the rule as ever is good seamanship and common sense.

CRIME CLASSIFICATIONS

So you had a run-in with the law—is it a felony or a misdemeanor? It's often hard to tell. In the past, crimes were always categorized as either a felony, a misdemeanor, or an infraction. For example, stealing was always a felony. However, this was reformed because it didn't account for the severity or intent of the crime, like stealing a loaf of bread versus stealing priceless diamonds. In the United States, crimes are classified by which courts see the cases and by the length of jail or prison time.

INFRACTIONS

Sometimes called a petty offense, an infraction is usually a violation of a civil code or traffic rule, not a criminal offense. Examples include minor traffic violations, jaywalking, or littering. A person usually receives a ticket and pays a fine. Sometimes a person will have to go to court.

MISDEMEANORS

A less serious criminal offense, a misdemeanor often results in fines, probation, and possible incarceration in a local or county jail. Offenses are typically separated into three classes: high or gross misdemeanors, ordinary misdemeanors, and petty misdemeanors. Examples of misdemeanors are first-time DUIs, reckless driving, public intoxication, prostitution, and retail theft.

FELONIES

This class of crime is the most serious offense, and is often classified by degrees, with a first-degree felony being the worst. The punishment if convicted can be a fine and jail time, often in a federal or state prison of more than a year, or, for more heinous crimes, execution. Examples of felonies include murder, arson, treason, kidnapping, and the sale and manufacture of drugs. After receiving a felony charge, a person often can't vote, buy guns, or gain certain types of employment.

OLYMPIAN GODS

The Greeks had a god or goddess for every natural phenomenon, abstract concept, and human emotion. They were ruled by the Olympian gods, who were led by the king and queen, Zeus and Hera. The Olympians descended from the Titans, who in turn descended from the primordial gods, born of original Chaos. Each generation fought the elder for power—Cronus fought and killed his father, Ouranos; Zeus fought and killed his father, Cronus. The fight between the Titans and the Olympians went on for ten years until Zeus prevailed and established his twelve-god pantheon on Mount Olympus.

1 PRIMORDIAL GODS BORN FROM CHAOS

Aether, Ananke, Chronos, Erebos, Eros, Gaia, Hemera, Hydros, Neboi, Nyx, Ouranos, Ourea, Phanes, Phusis, Pontus, Tartarus, Thalassa

Gaia (Earth) and **Ouranos** (sky) produced the Titans.

2 THE TITANS

Coeus, Crius, Cronus, Hyperion, Iapetus, Mnemosyne, Oceanus, Phoebe, Rhea, Tethys, Thea, Themis

Cronus (king of the Titans, god of devouring time) and **Rhea** (queen of heaven, goddess of female fertility and generation) produced the first generation of Olympian Gods.

3 THE OLYMPIAN GODS

Zeus, Hera, Demeter (goddess of agriculture), Poseidon (god of the sea and horses), Hades* (god of the underworld), Hestia** (goddess of hearth and home)

Zeus (god of the sky, king of the gods) and **Hera** (goddess of the female principle, queen of the gods) together and separately produced the second generation.

Ares (god of war), son of Zeus and Hera.

Apollo (god of prophecy, oracles, and music), son of Zeus and the Titaness Leto, twin to Artemis.

Artemis (goddess of the hunt and childbirth), daughter of Zeus and Leto, twin to Apollo.

HESIOD'S GENEALOGY

Most of what we know about Greek gods comes from *The Theogony* ("The Genealogy of the Gods") by the poet Hesiod (eighth–seventh century BC). It is an aggregation of all the contemporary local traditions, expressed in a narrative poem.

Aphrodite (goddess of love and desire), daughter of Zeus and Dione or created from sea foam.

Athena (goddess of wisdom and war), daughter of Zeus and Metis (daughter of Oceanus), born fully formed and armed from Zeus's head.

Hephaistos/Hephaestus (god of fire, smiths, and metalcraft), son of Hera.

Hermes (god of roads and travel, communication and thievery, messenger of the gods), son of Zeus and the star nymph Maia.

Dionysos/Dionysus (god of altered states), son of Zeus and the mortal Theban princess Semele, born from Zeus's thigh.

* Hades was not an Olympian resident, as he had his own realm below the earth.

** Hestia was later replaced by Dionysus as one of the twelve , while remaining one of the lesser Olympians.

PUTTING THE NORSE GODS IN THEIR PLACE

The Norse gods comprised three clans: the Aesir, the Vanir, and the Jötun. After a protracted war between the Aesir and the Vanir, in which the Aesir were dominant, a truce was called and hostages exchanged to ensure continued cooperation. The Aesir built Asgard, where they and their Vanir hostages lived. It was part of Midgard, the earthly realm in Norse mythology, linked to humanity by the rainbow bridge Bifröst. The remaining Vanir stayed in Vanaheim, and the Jötun, a race of giants, remained apart in Jötunheim, although Odin and Thor had liaisons with several giantesses.

THE GODS OF ASGARD

MAJOR AESIR GODS
Odin, Allfather, father of the gods.

Frigg, wife of Odin; queen of Asgard.

SONS OF ODIN
Thor, son of Frigg and Odin; god of the sky and thunder.

Baldur, son of Frigg and Odin; god of light, innocence, and beauty.

Vidar, son of Odin and the giantess Grid; god of vengeance.

Vali, son of Odin and the giantess Rind, born to avenge his brother Baldur.

OTHER MAJOR GODS
Bragi, husband to Idun, possible son of Odin; god of poetry.

Idun, wife of Bragi; goddess of youth and immortality.

Loki, son of the giant Farbáuti, foster brother of Odin; trickster god.

Hel, daughter of Loki; queen of the underworld.

Heimdall, guardian of Asgard; possibly a son of Odin.

Týr, god of combat and glory, son of the giant Hymir (or possibly Odin).

VANIR HOSTAGES
Njord, god of the sea.

Freyr, son of Njord; god of fertility.

MIGHTY MARVELOUS

Thor (and his mighty hammer, Mjöllnir) and Loki lead other lives as fictional superheroes in the Marvel Comic universe. And J. R. R. Tolkien famously drew some of his inspiration from Norse mythology for his *Lord of the Rings* saga.

Freya, daughter of Njord, twin to Freyr; goddess of love, beauty, death, and war.

MINOR AESIR GODS

Sif, wife of Thor, mother of the Valkyrie Thrud, Ull, and Modi.

Forseti, son of Baldur and Nanna; god of truth, peace, and justice.

Ull, son of Sif, stepson of Thor; god of hunting.

Hermod, son or servant of Odin; messenger of gods.

Hoenir, god of prophecy.

Hod, son of Odin, brother of Baldur; god of darkness.

Meili, son of Odin, brother of Thor.

Modi, the Angry, son of Thor and Sif.

Magni, the Strong, son of Thor and the giantess Járnsaxa.

Nanna, daughter of Nep, wife of Baldur.

Vili and Vé, brothers of Odin; cocreators of the first humans, Askr and Embla.

DEMONS

Demons weren't always considered a bad thing—in ancient Greek belief, a "daemon" was a lesser divinity or supernatural being, positioned, along with heroes and angels, somewhere between gods and humans. The Catholic Church, however, believes a demon to be a fallen angel under the command of Lucifer and destined to remain a demon for ever, because once a spiritual being has turned away from God, it cannot turn back. However, each demon is said to have an opposing saint in heaven, whose actions can negate those of the demon.

The sixteenth-century German bishop and theologian Peter Binsfeld proposed that seven of the demons—the seven Princes of Hell—tempt mankind to commit the traditional seven deadly sins. The offending demons are presented here in decreasing order of severity of their associated sins according to Dante's *Divine Comedy* (see page 112) completed in 1320.

LUCIFER (SIN: PRIDE)

The Emperor of Hell, who led a rebellion against God and as punishment was cast down from Heaven by the Archangel Michael, protector of the Church Militant. Lucifer is derived from the Latin *lux* ("light") + *fer* ("bearing"). Luciferianism is a belief system whose followers regard Lucifer as the bringer of light and wisdom.

LEVIATHAN (SIN: ENVY)

The Grand Admiral of Hell, portrayed as a great, whale-like sea monster, with the gates of Hell in his mouth. His description in the Book of Job depicts an alarming creature: "His sneezes flash forth light," "His breath kindles coals," and "His underparts are like sharp potsherds."

AMON (SIN: WRATH)

The Grand Marquis of Hell, who promotes hate and anger in the human heart. One of the lesser-known demons, Amon is depicted as a fire-breathing wolf with a serpent's tail, or as a man with a raven's head.

BELPHEGOR (SIN: SLOTH)

The Prince of Hell, portrayed as a horned demon (or sometimes an attractive young woman), who tempts the slothful with ideas for inventions that will bring them riches. Belphegor is said to be Hell's ambassador to France, and to haunt the Louvre in Paris.

MAMMON (SIN: GREED)

From the Aramaic māmōn, meaning "riches," Mammon is not so much a demon as a concept, although he is portrayed as a fallen angel in Milton's epic poem *Paradise Lost*, published in 1667. Mammon has come to be defined as "wealth regarded as a false object of worship": "Ye cannot serve God and Mammon."

BEELZEBUB (SIN: GLUTTONY)

The Prince of Demons, whose name translates from Hebrew as "Lord of the Flies." According to the Testament of Solomon, he entertained himself with activities such as bringing about destruction

A FALL FROM GRACE

According to the French inquisitor Sébastien Michaelis's 1613 classification (revealed to him, surprisingly, by a demon), demons belong to the corresponding choir of angels from which they fell. Four of the aforementioned demons —Lucifer, Leviathan, Beelzebub, and Asmodeus —are said to have belonged to the highest of the ninecelestial orders, Seraphim.

by means of tyrants, causing demons to be worshiped, and provoking jealousy and murder.

ASMODEUS (SIN: LUST)

The King of Hell, who delights in destroying marriages—killing off seven husbands of Sarah, the daughter of Raguel, the Angel of Justice, before being driven away, repelled by the odor of smoked fish liver. He is described as having three heads (the crowned head of a man, flanked by a bull and a ram), a serpent's tail, the feet of a goose, and flaming breath.

DIONYSIUS'S HIERARCHY OF ANGELS

After studying references to angels in the Scriptures and other sources, Pseudo-Dionysius The Areopagite, thought to have been a Syrian monk who lived around AD 500, compiled this hierarchy, which is still used today.

1 Seraphim
Also known as "the burning ones," since they are closest to God and radiate pure light. Often depicted with six wings, Seraphim glorify and praise God.

2 Cherubim
Originally depicted with four wings and four faces, they guard the gates of Eden. Today they are portrayed as cherubic babies with wings.

3 Thrones
They contemplate God's will in order to carry out His decisions.

SECOND SPHERE

4 Dominions
They carry out God's wishes and regulate the other angels.

5 Virtues
They encourage people to trust in God, often performing miracles to inspire this trust. The Virtues are associated with acts of heroism and help strengthen courage.

6 Powers
The Powers are viewed as the angels of birth and death. They also prevent the "fallen angels" from taking control and help humans overcome temptation.

THIRD SPHERE

7 Principalities
They protect against the invasion of evil angels and are the guardian angels of nations and rulers.

8 Archangels
They deliver God's messages to humans and command His armies of angels in the battle with the "sons of darkness."

9 Angels
The angels closest to humans, they are intermediaries between God and people. They pray for and guide humans.

THE ACADEMIC HIERARCHY OF THE GENRES

In the seventeenth century, the great European academies in Rome, Paris, and London established a hierarchy for painting that held sway for two centuries. André Félibien des Avaux, consultant to the French Académie Royale de Peinture et de Sculpture (Royal Academy of Painting and Sculpture), which held a central role in academic art, first announced the rankings in 1669. They were based on the belief in the Italian Renaissance that the highest form of art was the representation of the human form.

Man was the measure of all things, and the moral force of each genre played a key role. Size mattered, too, with the display value of each genre contributing to its place in the hierarchy. Still life ranked lowest, with the human figure performing acts of legendary or allegorical significance at the pinnacle, often nude or partially nude, as this was believed to demand the greatest artistic skill. The impressive scale of history painting meant such pieces were suitable for public spaces, for galleries and churches, and for large canvases, whereas the smaller sizes of still-life canvases made them more appropriate for domestic viewing. The top-down hierarchy was as follows:

---

1 HISTORY PAINTING (GRAND GENRE)
Large-scale narrative paintings of historical, classical, religious, mythological, and allegorical scenes. Heroic and noble deeds were portrayed and moral messages conveyed for the edification of the viewer.

2 PORTRAITURE OR PORTRAIT PAINTING
Scenes of heroic individuals, often larger than life, intended for public viewing, but also private portraiture.

3 GENRE PAINTING (*SCÈNES DE GENRE*)
Small-scale scenes of everyday life with ordinary people.

4 LANDSCAPES
Scenic views of the countryside, seas, rivers, mountains, and towns. The seventeenth-century Dutch art historian Samuel van Hoogstraten called landscapists "the common footmen in the army of art."

5 STILL LIFE
Arrangements of flowers, fruit, food, and everyday objects.

THE ORCHESTRA

Today's orchestra comprises four instrument families: strings (violins, violas, cellos, double basses), woodwind (flutes, oboes, clarinets, bassoons), brass (trumpets, trombones, tuba, French horns), and percussion (timpani, cymbals, triangle, xylophone). At the helm is the conductor (sometimes addressed as Maestro), who sets the tempo, ensures the entry of various instruments in the score, and shapes the music. Each section has its own leader.

STRINGS

First violins (*primo*)

Principal first violin—also orchestra leader/concert master.

Assistant concert master (replaces first violin in their absence, or there are two leaders).

Additional first violins—numbers vary, usually seated two to a stand/desk (hence "sitting second, third, fourth desk"); the player on the left generally turns the page.

The leader of the first violin section is the spokesperson for the rest of the orchestra and is second-in-command to the conductor, and as his or her right-hand (wo)man is usually seated to the conductor's left. He/she is the first point of contact between the conductor and the orchestra and liaises between the orchestra and its management. In the Baroque era orchestras were often led by the concertmaster.

Second violins (*secondo*)

(Usually play in lower registers than the first violins.)

Principal second violin.

Additional second violins—numbers vary, seating as per first violin.

OTHER SECTIONS

Each string section also has a principal player and follows the desk/stand system. There are principals, coprincipals, associate principals, and subprincipals within a section, and the number depends on the size of the section and on the size and wealth of the orchestra. Other instrumental groups also generally have a principal. The orchestra is, however, an essentially democratic body.

PIANO

The piano is a solo instrument and not part of the general orchestra. It is brought onstage for a particular piece and its position is determined by the conductor, who can also decide the seating arrangements for the entire orchestra.

CONTEMPORARY SYMPHONY ORCHESTRA

The composition of today's symphony orchestra remains much as it was in the late nineteenth century, with typically thirty violins, twelve violas, ten cellos, eight double basses, four of each woodwind, eight horns, four trumpets, three trombones, one tuba, and several percussion instruments. Numbers vary according to the piece being played and the demands of the score. For example, Shostakovich's Fourth Symphony requires six flutes.

THE BALLET COMPANY

Most classical ballet companies have a hierarchy, but structure and rigidity, and job titles, vary between companies and countries. Early ballet companies such as the Paris Opera Ballet and the Mariinsky Ballet in St. Petersburg, Russia, established a basic structure of seniority, which has evolved in different ways in companies around the world. Different hierarchies for male and female dancers have now merged into a gender-neutral classification. In the nineteenth and very early twentieth centuries some companies revolved around a single star ballerina, but rosters today include several principal dancers. Some appoint a principal guest artist—Sylvie Guillem and Carlos Acosta both held this title with the Royal Ballet in London. Smaller companies, unfettered by the constraints of boards of directors or government funding requirements, can devise their own structure to suit their repertoire and size. Some are completely egalitarian, and all the dancers are named as part of the group.

In major companies in the UK and Europe, the structure might be:

ARTISTIC DIRECTOR
Often a retired dancer, he or she makes casting decisions, schedules programs, commissions choreographers (and may also choreograph themselves), and hires and fires dancers. In major companies the artistic director reports to a board of governors and, ultimately, to the government minister or official in charge of arts and culture.

ASSISTANT ARTISTIC DIRECTOR
Supports the artistic director and monitors rehearsals and standards.

BALLET MASTERS AND REPETITEURS
Usually give the daily classes and direct rehearsals. Repetiteurs are responsible for coaching dancers in individual roles and for ensuring that the choreographer's intentions are adhered to.

PRINCIPAL DANCERS

The highest rank within the company, they usually appear in leading roles (e.g., Aurora and the Prince in *The Sleeping Beauty*). In the Paris Opera Ballet they are known as *danseur étoile* (literally "star dancer").

PRINCIPAL CHARACTER ARTISTS

Dancers who perform important character roles in a ballet.

FIRST SOLOISTS AND SOLOISTS

Dancers who perform solo and minor roles (e.g., the Lilac Fairy in *The Sleeping Beauty*) and can also understudy the principal role.

FIRST ARTISTS OR CORYPHÉES

The more senior members of the corps de ballet.

CORPS DE BALLET ("BODY OF THE BALLET")

Comprises male and female dancers who dance as an ensemble, as one body, with synchronized movements. There is also a ranking structure within the corps de ballet, usually based on the length of service (first year corps, second year corps, and so on). In the United States, major companies are usually structured as follows:

Principal dancers
Soloists
Corps de ballet
Apprentices—*usually young dancers straight out of school, who are hired on a yearly or seasonal basis so that the artistic staff can watch how they develop.*

In Russia, the structure is usually:

Principal dancers
Leading soloists
First soloists
Soloists
Coryphées
Corps de ballet

Large Russian companies also have a parallel company of character dancers.

ABSOLUTELY EXCEPTIONAL

The term *Prima Ballerina Assoluta* is an exceptional title awarded to a ballerina who has been an integral part of a company's success. Margot Fonteyn was Prima Ballerina Assoluta at the Royal Ballet and to date remains the only dancer to be awarded the honor by the company.

MUSIC SALES

In February 1942, the American record label RCA Victor awarded Glenn Miller and His Orchestra a gold record to celebrate the sale of 1.2 million copies of the still instantly recognizable song "Chattanooga Choo Choo," starting a music sales success ranking that is still going strong today. Certification originally related to sales of a physical single or album, but now with the advent of new technology, there are also awards for sales of digital downloads and even phone ringtones.

UNITED STATES

In the USA, sales awards are certified by the Recording Industry Association of America (RIAA). The criteria in terms of numbers of physical albums and downloads sold are currently:

ALBUMS
Gold: 500,000 copies
Platinum: 1 million copies
Multiplatinum: More than 2 million
Diamond: More than 10 million

DOWNLOADS
Gold: 100,000
Platinum: 200,000
Multiplatinum: 400,000, then increments of 200,000

THRILLING FIGURES
Michael Jackson's 1982 album *Thriller* holds the Guinness World Record for the world's best-selling album, and has been certified twenty-nine times platinum by the RIAA. It shares the title of best-selling album in the USA with the Eagles' *Their Greatest Hits*.

In the UK, sales awards are certified by the British Phonographic Industry. The criteria in terms of numbers of albums sold* are currently:

Silver: 60,000
Gold: 100,000
Platinum: 300,000
Multiplatinum: Multiples of 300,000

*1,000 streams count as equivalent to 1 album sale

QUEEN OF HITS

In July 2016, the UK's Official Albums Chart celebrated its sixtieth birthday and confirmed Queen's 1981 album *Greatest Hits* as the nation's best seller to date, as it sold over six million copies in the UK.

Achieving a sales award from Music Canada appears less challenging than in the neighboring United States—but its population is only 10 percent of that of the United States, which is reflected in the criteria for certification, currently:

ALBUMS
Gold: 40,000
Platinum: 80,000
Diamond: 800,000
Double diamond: 1,600,000

RINGTONES
Gold: 20,000
Platinum: 40,000
Diamond: 400,000
Double diamond: 800,000

The best-selling album worldwide by a Canadian artist is Shania Twain's *Come On Over*, at thirty-nine million copies.

DECIBEL SCALE

The human ear can perceive an enormous range of sound levels. A logarithmic scale was created to express levels of sound. The levels are measured in decibels (dB), which range from 0, which is the quietest sound a healthy ear can detect, increasing in increments of 3 for each doubling in sound intensity, until around 130, where sound intensity becomes painful. Following are some examples of sound decibel levels:

Breathing **10 dB**

Rustling Leaves **20 dB**

Birdsong **44 dB**

Quiet conversation **50 dB**

Air conditioner at 100 feet **60 dB**

Vacuum cleaner **70 dB**

Blender **88 dB**

Power lawn mower **96 dB**

Live rock concert **108–114 dB**

Police siren **120 dB**

Aircraft carrier deck **140 dB**

FILM CLASSIFICATION IN THE USA

The Motion Picture Association of America (MPAA) rates films. The ratings have no legal force, and filmmakers have no obligation to have their film rated before it is released. States can apply their own laws. Films are rated for violence, language, substance abuse, nudity, and sex. The Classification and Rating Administration (CARA) regulates the system. The MPAA also rates trailers and advertising material. TV and video games are rated by other bodies.

These are the current ratings, as established in the 1990s:

G (GENERAL AUDIENCE)
Suitable for all ages.

PG (PARENTAL GUIDANCE SUGGESTED)
Some material may not be suitable for children.

PG13 (PARENTAL GUIDANCE STRONGLY CAUTIONED)
Some material may not be suitable for children under thirteen.

R (RESTRICTED)
Children under seventeen need an accompanying parent or adult guardian.

NC-17 (ADULTS ONLY)
No one aged seventeen or under.

NR (NOT RATED)
Films that have not been submitted for rating.

UR (UNRATED)
Films that have not been submitted; or uncut, recut, or extended versions of films that may have been rated.

TRAILERS AND ADVERTISING MATERIAL

GREEN—when the trailer accompanies a similarly rated film.

YELLOW—for films on the internet only, rated PG13 or stronger.

RED—the trailer is restricted, suitable for previewing before R and NC-17 films only.

THIS FILM HAS NOT BEEN RATED—displayed in trailers if the film is unrated.

GOLF

Golf has a partly bird-themed hierarchy to denote how well or otherwise a player performs in relation to the par rating of a hole (usually, eighteen holes per golf course). Unusually, this hierarchy extends both upward and downward from a center point—par.

DEEP DESPAIR

Triple bogey—three strokes above par

Double bogey—two strokes above par

Bogey—one stroke above par (e.g., a score of four on a par-three hole)

Par—the number of strokes a scratch player (expert, handicap zero) normally requires to complete the hole

Birdie—one stroke under par (birdie = "awesome" in early twentieth-century American slang)

Eagle—two strokes under par

Albatross (British)/double eagle (American)—three strokes under par

UTTER EUPHORIA

Condor—four under par (unofficial and extremely rare, for example, a hole-in-one on a par-five hole, drinks all around at the nineteenth hole, or clubhouse)

THE ENGLISH MEN'S FOOTBALL LEAGUE

English men's football (soccer) teams are organized into a pyramid of interconnected leagues. It is based on a system of promotion and relegation that depends on points gathered throughout a season. Theoretically any team can climb to the top, or sink down to the bottom.

There are more than 140 football leagues in England, but the top eleven are the most significant. The first is the self-governing Premier League, established in 1992 by a breakaway group of the top teams of what was then the First Division. The English Football League (established 1888) runs levels two, three, and four. The National League System (NLS), answerable to the Football Association (FA), runs levels five to eleven.

PREMIER LEAGUE
Level One
The Premier League
Twenty clubs
Nationwide
Full-time professional
Self-funding corporation,
not sponsored

ENGLISH FOOTBALL LEAGUE
Level Two
The English Football League:
the Championship
Twenty-four clubs
Nationwide
Full-time professional
Commercially sponsored

Level Three
The English Football League:
League One
Twenty-four clubs
Nationwide
Full-time professional
Commercially sponsored

Level Four
The English Football League:
League Two
Twenty-four clubs
Nationwide
Full-time professional
Commercially sponsored

LEAGUE AND NONLEAGUE

Confusingly, the National League
System clubs are known as
nonleague, because they were
not part of the original English
Football League.

NATIONAL LEAGUE
Level Five
National League
Twenty-four clubs
Nationwide
Professional and semiprofessional
Commercially sponsored

Level Six
*(All Level Six leagues are
of equal status)*
National League North
Twenty-two clubs
Regional
Professional and
semiprofessional
Commercially sponsored

Level Six
National League South
Twenty-two clubs
Regional
Professional and semiprofessional
Commercially sponsored

Level Seven
*(All Level Seven leagues
are of equal status)*
Northern Premier League
North of England and North Wales
Premier Division
Twenty-four clubs
Semiprofessional and amateur
Commercially sponsored

Level Seven
Southern Football League
Midlands, South and Southwest
England, South Wales
Premier Division
Twenty-four clubs
Semiprofessional and amateur
Commercially sponsored

Level Seven
Isthmian League
London and Southeast England
Premier Division
Twenty-four clubs
Semiprofessional and amateur
Commercially sponsored

Level Eight
(All Level Eight leagues are of equal status)

Northern Premier League
North of England and North Wales
Division One North
Twenty-two clubs
Semiprofessional and amateur
Commercially sponsored

Level Eight
Northern Premier League
North of England and North Wales
Division One South
Twenty-two clubs
Semiprofessional and amateur
Commercially sponsored

Level Eight
Southern Football League
Midlands, South and Southwest England, South Wales
Division One Central
Twenty-two clubs
Semiprofessional and amateur
Commercially sponsored

Level Eight
Southern Football League
Midlands, South and Southwest England, South Wales
Division One South & West
Twenty-two clubs
Semiprofessional and amateur
Commercially sponsored

Level Eight
Isthmian League
London and Southeast England
Division One North
Twenty-four clubs
Semiprofessional and amateur

Level Eight
Isthmian League
London and Southeast England
Division One South
Twenty-four clubs
Semiprofessional and amateur

Level Nine
Top divisions from fourteen leagues round the country in parallel
Nineteen to twenty-three clubs per division
Semiprofessional and amateur

Level Ten
First divisions, with some premier divisions, from seventeen leagues around the country in parallel
Fourteen to twenty-two clubs per division
Semiprofessional and amateur

Level Eleven
First divisions, with some premier divisions, from forty-three leagues around the country in parallel
Fourteen to twenty clubs per division
Semiprofessional and amateur

FOOTBALL NUMBERS BY POSITION

In 1973, the National Football League standardized the jersey number that players in positions could wear, a variation of which was adopted by both high school and college football. This enabled officials on the field to determine quickly if a player is doing something not allowed by their position.

All players must have the numbers between 1 and 99, with no two players on the same team having the same number allowed on the field at the same time.

1-19
quarterbacks, wide receivers, punters, kickers

20-49
running backs, defensive backs

50-59
defensive lineman, centers

60-79
defensive linemen, offensive linemen

80-89
receivers, tight ends

90-99
defensive linemen, linebackers

Some numbers are considered better than others. For example, 32 has been a favorite of running backs, including Edgerrin James, Jim Brown, and Franco Harris. The legendary quarterbacks, including Joe Namath, Terry Bradshaw, Roger Staubach, and Jim Kelly, have sported number 12.

CHESS PIECES

The game begins with two "armies" of sixteen chess pieces facing each other across the board in order of ascending rank. Each piece is assigned a point value, which does not affect the game but allows players to evaluate the risk of loss. The aim is to trap your opponent's king in checkmate so that it cannot escape by moving, blocking, or capturing your threatening piece. Game over.

So that the moves can be recorded, each of the sixty-four squares on the board has a grid number. The eight squares across the board run from *a* to *h*, from left to right. The squares down the board run from 1 to 8, from bottom to top. The board is set up so that for each player, the bottom far right corner contains a white square.

The pieces in order of value are:

KING | QUEEN | ROOK

Starting place on board: fourth in from the right in the back row, always on a square of opposite color (e8 black king; e1 white king).

Value: priceless.

Moves: only one square, but in any direction (forward, backward, sideways, diagonally).

Illegal moves: the king must not put himself in check.

Starting place on board: fourth in from the left in the back row, always on a square of the same color as herself (d8 black queen, d1 white queen).

Value: nine points.

Moves: as far as is wanted in a straight line forward, backward, sideways, and diagonally; if she captures a piece, the move is over.

Illegal moves: the queen may not move through her own pieces.

Starting place on board: the two rooks stand at either end of the back row (a8 and h8 black rooks, a1 and h1 white rooks).

Value: five points.

Moves: as far as is wanted forward, backward, and sideways.

BISHOP

KNIGHT

PAWN

Starting place on board: one on each side of the king and queen in the back row (c8 and f8 black; c1 and f1 white).

Value: three points.

Moves: as far as is wanted, diagonally only; must always stay on the color on which it began.

Starting place on board: one on each side of each bishop in the back row (b8 and g8 black; b1 and g1 white).

Value: three points.

Moves: in an L shape, two squares in one direction, and then one at a ninety-degree angle; the only piece that can move over other pieces.

Starting place on board: eight pawns, one in each square of the second row (a7–h7 black, a2–h2 white).

Value: one point.

Moves: forward or backward, two squares on the first move, one square per move after that; can take only pieces diagonally in front of them.

Additional powers: if a pawn makes it to the opposing back row, it can redeem any one of its side's pieces that have been captured; this is how a captured queen can be rescued.

ILLUSTRATIONS

Shutterstock.com: Vitaly Ilyasov p. 10-11; Rvector p. 12; galbera p. 13; Viktorija Reuta p. 14; PPVector p. 15; Katason p.16; Billy Read p.17; In-Finity p. 21; Neungstockr p. 22; jesadaphorn p. 23; mckenna71 p. 26; Dzm1try p. 27; drvector p. 29; BUTENKOV ALEKSEI p. 30; Verkhozina Ekaterina p. 32; Robert Biedermann p. 33; Filip Bjorkman p. 34; Zsschreiner p. 34-35; stas11 p. 38; cmgirl p.40-41; Top Vector Studio p. 42-43; Finland p. 44; Pictogram studio p. 46; Martial Red p. 47; Sri Rejeki p. 48; vector twins p. 49; Chambliss1 p. 50; johavel p. 52; Rashad Ashurov p. 56; cidepix p. 58; BigAlBaloo p. 61; vectortatu p. 62; Tata Donets p. 63; Dzm1try p. 64; Mediterraneo7 p. 66; HN Works p. 67; Antiwar p. 68; Miceking p. 70; Olha Yerofieieva p. 71; lana_elanor p. 72-73; Champ008 p. 74; Makalo86 p. 75; moibalkon p. 76; Macrovector p. 78-79; Nadya_Art p. 80-81; Martial Red p. 83; Marnikus p. 84; Miceking p. 85; MarShot p. 86-87; COOL STUFF p. 88; Kilroy79 p. 89; Marie Nimrichterova p. 90; PeoGeo p. 92; robuart p. 95; trgrowth p. 96-97; Nevada31 p. 98; Alice in Wonderland p. 99; udaix p. 100-101; MaxterDesign p. 102-103; Vector Tradition SM p. 104-105; Eugenia Bobrov p. 106-107; Stock Vector p. 108; Irina Medvedev Mejg p. 109; Kisan p. 110; pupahava p. 112-115; wanpatsorn p. 117; merion_merion p. 119; Coolgraphic p. 120-121; Vector FX p. 122; marymyyr p. 125; Dimes p. 126; Jennie p. 128; TRONIN ANDREI p. 131; Cube29 p. 132-134; Findriyani p. 136; Antonina Tsyganko p. 137; Anastasia_B p. 138; VooDoo13 p. 140; Alexandr III p. 142-143; VikiVector p. 145; VLADGRIN p. 147; Bonezboyz p. 149; paramouse p. 150; Petrovich Igor p. 151; Vdant85 p. 152; marysuperstudio p. 156; Borodatch p. 159; VoodooDot p. 160; Lukas Stefanski p. 161; Eugene Ivanov p. 162-163; Alexzel p. 165-166; LWY Partnership p. 167; Master p. 168; ARCHITECTEUR p. 172; Glinskaja Olga p. 176; Rauf Aliyev p. 177; NatBasil p. 178; Svetlana Maslova p. 179; still p. 180; Bobnevv p. 180-181; Dzianis_Rakhuba p. 182; Sergey Mastepanov p. 185; Denys Koltovskyi p. 189

Dreamstime.com: Jolita Marcinkene p. 164; Arcadia Ivanchenko p. 171; John Takai p. 174; Murphy81 p.184; Burlesck p. 190-191